THE FIRST QUESTIONS

COACHING YOUR WAY TO LEADERSHIP SUCCESS

RON HURST

ISBN: 978-1-4834-1203-0 (sc)
ISBN: 978-1-4834-1202-3 (e)

Library of Congress Control Number: 2014908349

Lulu Publishing Services rev. date: 5/8/2014

Dedicated to my mom, Cecelia E. Hurst, who valiantly fought cancer for more than eleven years. You are the bravest person and leader I was blessed to know and love. Now that the fight is over, I wish you peace and rest in the arms of your Savior. We will meet again.

Acknowledgments

You never really write a book alone, and this effort is no different. I am indebted to my wife, Kim, and children Mitch and Meg for putting up with the process. Thank you to Daryn Schiveley, who helped draw out of me the material for the last chapters and transcribe many pages of notes. Thanks also to Kristel Faye Soriano, who helped with the first several chapters. There are many stories embedded in this book, and these come from so many wonderful people I have met along the way. There are too many to name, but thank you to all. You made my journey richer and this book deeper and more powerful.

Special thanks to Lulu Publishing for helping me complete this project.

Contents

Introduction

Early in my career I was drawn to observe how others led. I did not like what I saw. Most of the people in management positions with the authority to lead really did not appear to know what it meant to lead. It wasn't so much that they were negligent or reckless; rather, it appeared they simply didn't know a better way. I saw too many cases where people were hurt by managers doing what the managers thought was the right thing but were doing it in the wrong way. Never one to criticize without the willingness of a person attempting to do better, I set about the task of becoming a competent leader. Throughout my career I took on and mastered levels of management in different contexts. Whether I was an engineer, supervisor, technical sales manager, quality manager, an operations manager, a plant manager, or president, I have committed to a journey of learning along the way.

Several years, positions, and degrees later, I found myself studying for what I knew would ultimately be the answer to a career-defining question: "How can I help people lead better?"

I was attending Fielding Graduate School, studying in their evidence-based coaching program. The answer to this question was to weave a healthy dose of coaching questions into experiential training programs, essentially transforming the process into group leadership coaching. The mix of one-on-one coaching and group coaching led to this book and to the success my company has enjoyed in Southern California.

Since graduating Fielding, I founded the company Developing Leaders Inc. and now help thousands of people in Southern California and beyond to become great leaders. We offer training/group coaching programs to help aspiring and existing managers increase their leadership competence.

This is a book designed to help you grow your leadership ability. Each chapter will lead you through a series of topics related to your own skills. It will help you discover who you are and how to leverage your strengths. The format is a series of questions related to key topics that I have found critical to my coaching clients. In many areas, you can complete exercises to further your learning and growth.

Each chapter will explore a different aspect of your growth as a leader. Chapter 1, Personal Mastery, focuses on you, looking deeply at who you are and your worldview. How does your self-perception hold you back or facilitate your success? With knowledge of self we can begin to interact with the world in a purposeful and wise manner. It is here we begin to discover our purpose and begin to walk in it. Chapter 2, Purpose Mastery, follows with an exploration of what you want to accomplish as a leader.

Chapter 3 looks at Change Mastery. I cannot tell you how often this area is mishandled by people in leadership roles. The ability to lead people through change is difficult, yes, but so necessary. It is built upon a foundation of trust and authentic relationship. Chapter 4 continues with an exploration of Interpersonal Mastery, or how you interact with the world around you.

Chapter 5 is about action. How do you act in an appropriate and sustainable way? Leadership requires action. In the absence of action, a leader is nothing but a dreamer or thinker. Chapter 6, Motivation Mastery, is an exploration of how you motivate yourself to achieve.

Whether you have a belief in an Almighty God or perhaps hold a different set of spiritual beliefs, the concept of faith cannot be ignored. Recognize that many of your followers want to believe in something, to have hope in a cause bigger than themselves. The final chapter, Faith Mastery, is really a way of bringing all these concepts together and closing out with the realization that "leaders are dealers in hope" (Napoleon Bonaparte).

How Is This Book Designed?

This is a straightforward book, a coaching book. It is set up to ask you the first question in a line of thinking to help you discover your leadership abilities. It's what you would get if you were sitting face to face with me in a live coaching session. These are my starting questions.

Of course they are, as the title suggests, "the first questions" in a number of different topic areas. If you follow the threads and answer each question honestly, you will learn much about yourself.

I have to be honest with you. There is no second question without some level of interaction. Certainly you could come up with your own second questions, and I encourage you to do so. You can learn much through the reflective/active process of professional leadership coaching.

Why Should You Read This Book?

Perhaps you heard of the Peter Principle. Originally identified by Dr. Laurence J. Peter in 1969, it relates the idea that people are continually promoted until they reach their level of incompetence. This concept, while sarcastic and bitter in tone, is truer than most of us care to admit. Consider the talented work associate who is promoted to team lead or the hard-driving engineer who becomes manager. They were productive and great in their previous positions, but what does their productivity have to do with leading a group?

Unfortunately, there is little correlation between technical abilities to perform tasks well and the ability to lead a group. There are specific skills that will help you be an effective leader, and this book is designed to help you find and then practice them. I don't want you to become a victim of the Peter Principle. You can learn to lead, starting now.

How Do Organizations Determine Who Will Get Promoted into Leadership/Management Positions?

Often they choose people who are confident and competent in their current role. What does their current role have to do with leadership? Often not much: unfortunately, well-meaning managers mistake confidence and task competence for overall confidence and competence. They must reason that a resourceful and capable employee will be able to figure out the leadership role. Many a promising career has been derailed over this simplistic assumption. In my career I have too often seen a talented employee who was promoted, failed in the new role, and was fired or demoted. What a tragedy! This should not happen. Do not let this happen to you. If you learn to navigate the skill set a leader needs, you will greatly improve your probability of success.

In March 1956, Robert Katz wrote an article titled "Skills of an Effective Administrator" for the *Harvard Business Review* that defined this issue. At the employee level, we are rewarded for our technical skill. Our ability to complete specific tasks, often-repetitive ones, becomes our world. When we move into a leadership role, suddenly there is a specific and significant need for interpersonal skill.

Leadership requires a different skill set than that necessary for an employee to succeed. The leader's skill set involves a healthy dose of interpersonal skills, conceptual abilities, and technical expertise. My intent is to help you think about who you are and how you are equipped to lead so you can develop excellence in leadership.

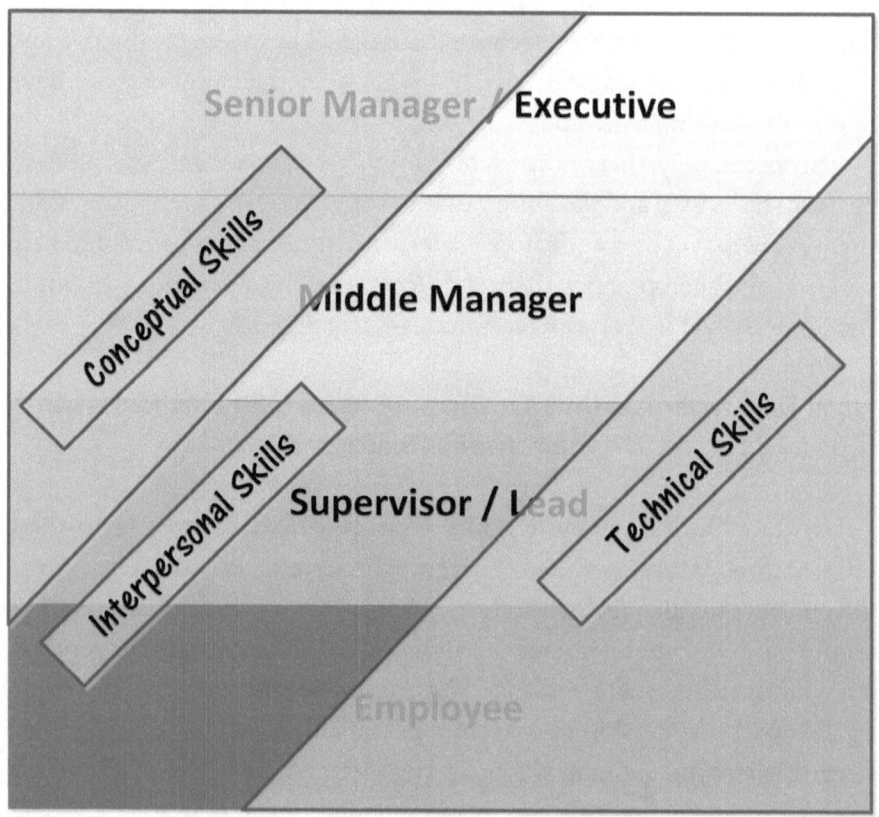

Leadership is about many things, and there is no one recipe for leadership success. Leadership is a dynamic and creative process of matching abilities with context and need. Real leadership starts with an understanding of self and the way you interact with your environment. For this reason, we begin with the concept of personal mastery.

Enjoy,
Ron

CHAPTER 1
Personal Mastery

The only person you are destined
to become is the person you decide
to be.—Ralph Waldo Emerson

Questions of Identity

Where do you lead from?

In his book *Leadership from the inside Out,* Kevin Cashman relates the story of a priest on an evening stroll in pre-revolutionary Russia.

The priest was challenged by a solider. "Halt! Who are you? Where are you going? What's your purpose here?"

The priest considered the challenge for several moments before replying, "If I pay you, will you ask me that every day?"

Who are you?

Where are you going?

What's your purpose here?

Those questions are something a leader should be able to answer at any given moment.

In Greek mythology, the Oracle at Delphi said, "Know thyself." It is important to know yourself and where you're coming from. When you know that foundation, you can lead from wisdom, patience, and peace, as opposed to reaction and emotion.

Who are you?

My company, Developing Leaders Inc., maintains a website (http://developingleaders.co/). On the site is a basic training exercise in awareness building that will help you become aware of yourself and those around you.

The module is based on a concept from the discipline of neuro-linguistic programming (NLP) called *perceptual position*. The idea is that all of us operate and interact with the world from a number of perspectives or positions. The model addresses the frame of mind we are in as we interact with others.

When thinking about the three perceptual positions, or frames of mind, our focus can be on self-need (first position), awareness of others (second position), and/or from the point of view of a detached observer (third position). The training module has been used to help leaders gain increased awareness in the moment. Increased awareness leads to better choices when faced with difficult situations.

Here is how the training exercise works.

Perceptual Position Exercise

Objective: Through firsthand experience, learn to recognize and identify each of the three perceptual positions.
Materials: You will need some basic office products: sticky notes or name tag labels and colored pens or markers work well.
Setup: Each participant will need three stickers. Write number 1 in red on one sticker, write 2 in blue on the next, and write 3 in green on the third.

Separate participants into groups of three people. Identify two members to volunteer to be in first position for the first exercise. The remaining member will remain in third position. Be sure to place your sticker with the correct number on your shoulder so everyone knows what position you are in.

Have the two members in first position discuss something exciting that happened to them in the last week. The remaining member observes only. The two members in first person will, if correctly in first position, spend more time focused on what they want to say than on what the other person is attempting to tell them. Over talking one another or going back and forth in a one-upmanship manner is common here. Allow the conversation to continue for up to approximately five minutes.

Debrief:

When you debrief the exercise, follow the questions.

1. What happened?
2. What emotions did you experience?
3. How did those emotions affect your approach to the exercise?
4. How effective were your interactions with other members?
5. What can you do differently in the future?

Note that you will want to allow members in both perceptual positions to answer these questions.

The members in first position will likely not recall much, if any, of what the other member spoke about. They were so focused on themselves they were not really listening to the other person. Many will be frustrated by this exchange. Others will recognize this pattern of non-communication as something they experience now. Regardless of the emotional reaction, they will see how ineffective communication is between people whose frame of mind is self-focused.

Repeat Exercise

Setup

Have participants switch places; the observer goes to first position, the other two members take one each of second and third position. Be sure to place your sticker with the correct number on your shoulder so everyone knows what position you are in.

Repeat the exercise and the debrief. In this case, you will notice the speaking volume is much lower and there is a noticeable drop in tension in the room. The conversation seems smooth and natural.

Teaching Point:

These two exercises illustrate the difference between ineffective and effective communication. They create an artificial scenario in which the participant can become aware of one of the reasons communication does not work. The reason relates directly to a lack of self-awareness. When we speak from a self-focused place without regard to the other person, we may be effectively ignoring social clues and speaking from a low-awareness state.

The ability to recognize the perceptual position of the other person in the exchange provides us with a critical ability to gain awareness in the moment. When the thought in our head says, *Oh they are in first position. That's why I am getting frustrated with this conversation,* we then have an excellent opportunity to ask ourselves, "Where am I? What position am I in right now? Is that where I want to be?" This ability gives us the opportunity to make a conscious choice of our frame of mind in the moment and hence be self-aware.

So what did you learn about yourself in this exercise? I encourage you to take a few moments and jot down your thoughts.

The process of building self-awareness is one of daily discipline and repetition and will substantially aid your growth as a leader. Continuing on the building of self-awareness, we turn our attention to building awareness of our strengths and abilities.

Questions of Character

How would you describe your character?
What aspects of your character are you most proud of?

As you work through these questions, consider what experiences have led you to become proud of that characteristic. The story here is important.

Often the ability to associate experiences with positive memories and emotions builds our confidence and further develops us.

Several years ago I experienced this when a major automotive manufacturing company and customer experienced a costly defect involving the product my company supplied. As a supervisor responsible for problem-solving customer complaints, I was flown in to help with the situation. The general manager of the automotive plant explained when I arrived that the defect was costing his facility more than a million dollars a day. In a not so subtle way he made it clear that if my company's product was to blame, we would be paying a costly bill. Leveraging my problem-solving skills and with the support of my team, we were quickly able to derive the root cause and eliminate the defect. It turned out the defect was a result of a chemical contaminant that had built up in another supplier's product. The chemical contaminant had caused corrosion of my company's product, leading to the defect.

Completing this investigation was instrumental in improving our company's standing with our customer and gave me a significant boost in my confidence in solving challenging manufacturing problems. Today when a challenging problem comes up, I draw upon a deep reserve of experience on difficult challenges and my ability to problem solve. Instead of fearing such situations, I welcome them. I find them exciting!

How do you rate your personal confidence?

Fascinatingly, people follow those who are confident, sometimes to their own detriment, even if leaders have no idea where they are headed or have no moral compass and lead their followers in tragic directions. A leader needs more than confidence, certainly. It is important, though, that we understand how crucial confidence is. Think about the last time you asked a sales clerk for technical help with a significant purchase. If the clerk spoke hesitantly, stuttered over details, made minimal eye contact, or said "I don't know" too many times, what would your reaction be? Going to the next store or at least the next clerk is my guess.

If you find you rate your confidence low, this is important to explore. I recommend you find small ways to grow it. Put yourself in situations that require you to take action. It could be something as simple as answering a coworker's question that you would normally be silent on. Choose something small; give yourself an opportunity to grow in this important area.

What are you about?

This is such an important place to start! Who are you really? Do you take the time to understand who you are and how others perceive you? Have you done a personal inventory, and do you understand the areas that are potential liabilities for you? How about your core strengths? Do you know them? These are important because they form a foundation we will build on. Do not skimp here; be real. No one but you will judge you on this. Knowing where to start is crucial to your progress.

To help you, the following is a list of sample strengths and liabilities.

Sample Strengths	Sample Liabilities
Organization	Indecisiveness
Critical Thinking	Quick Temper
Communication	Insensitivity
Problem Solving	Selfishness
Detail Orientation	Poor judgment
Personal Discipline	Distractibility
Initiative	Uncooperative
Tenacity	Inflexibility
Integrity	Controlling Nature
Learning Oriented	Unmotivated

Let's look at the first strength and the first liability. If we are well organized, we will have the ability to ensure important priorities are handled in a timely manner. We will show up on time for meetings prepared to deal with the issue at hand.

In contrast, indecisiveness can be a significant liability. When a decision needs to be made and we lack needed information, an indecisive person may delay, stall, or otherwise not make a decision. A decisive person will weigh the pros and cons of the potential decision and make the best choice with the available information. As a leader, being organized and decisive is a definite advantage.

Strengths

In my travels, I have encountered numerous people who cannot answer the question of personal strengths and liabilities. Whether it stems from a lack of reflection or a lack of confidence, not knowing your strengths is a surefire way *not* to grow. Embracing and growing your strengths and shoring up your liabilities should be a daily discipline.

We can appreciate the perspective Curt Coffman and Marcus Buckingham offer in their book *First Break All the Rules*. They define a talent as "a recurring pattern of thought, feeling, or behavior that can be productively applied" (71). A talent, yes, but the way they define how great managers think closely fits with what I describe as strengths. What comes almost effortlessly to you that you can repeat with positive outcomes?

Questions of Value

When asked, "What are your values?," many would answer, "I don't know my values." If that's your answer, it's time to start uncovering your values.

What do you value?

Developing Leaders Inc. offers an excellent exercise to walk you through the process of discovering your values. To complete the exercise follow the instructions below.

Values Exercise

Objective: Through introspection, determine your personal values.

Materials: You will need a copy of the list of potential values and a pair of scissors.

Setup: Each participant will need a copy of the potential values. Cut the potential value list into individual strips of paper. This list was obtained from www.mindtools.com/pages/article/newTED_85.htm.

Potential Values			
Accuracy	Achievement	Adventurousness	Altruism
Ambition	Balance	Being the best	Belonging
Boldness	Challenge	Commitment	Community
Compassion	Contentment	Cooperation	Correctness
Creativity	Curiosity	Decisiveness	Dependability
Determination	Discipline	Expertise	Expressiveness
Fairness	Faith	Family-oriented	Fitness Health
Focus	Freedom	Fun Enjoyment	Generosity
Growth	Happiness Joy	Hard Work	Honesty
Honor	Humility	Independence	Ingenuity
Intelligence	Intellectual Status	Intuition	Justice
Leadership	Loyalty	Mastery	Obedience
Openness	Originality	Preparedness	Professionalism
Quality-orientation	Reliability	Restraint	Results-oriented
Sensitivity	Service	Simplicity	Soundness
Spontaneity	Stability	Structure	Success
Support	Timeliness	Traditionalism	Understanding
Uniqueness	Vision		

As you read each of the seventy potential values from the table, separate them into two groups. On the right, place those potential values you like, that are positive in some way. On the left, include those potential values you do not connect with, those you do not like or have no opinion on. Considering the group to your right you should have only thirty of the original list remaining when this step is complete.

Read each potential value from the group you liked (the group to your right), this time paying attention to how they make you feel. If you sense a positive emotion, place it to your right. Discard those that have a negative or neutral connection. When complete you should now have only fifteen potential values that you have a positive connection with.

Finally we will sort the remaining fifteen positive potential values. In this pass be sure to sit comfortably and take several deep cleansing breaths before beginning. Release any tension in your body and clear your mind. Now read each potential value, paying particular attention to your body's and mind's reaction to each. Create a group of those values that evoke a positive emotion or paint a positive picture in your mind's eye. When you are done you should have only six to eight cards remaining.

With each of these cards you are encouraged to draft a statement that explains what each means to you. This list will give you a fair start at better understanding your values.

As we move on to the next question, you will have the opportunity to further understand how these values guide your actions and decisions.

What story can you tell me that can bring one of your values to life?

The more a person repeats his or her values and puts a story to it, the more real these values become. What happens is that the value moves from being a concept or vague idea to a concrete reality.

From the early days of my career I knew integrity was an absolute core value. I knew I must behave in such a way as to be able to look myself in the eye the next day regardless of my actions. Since I knew lying, cheating, and stealing, amongst other actions, would mean not looking myself in the eye, I would never do any of these.

It was a clear concept in my head for quite a while—until one day my manager asked me to cover for him so he could skip a mandatory meeting. He said, "Just tell them our meeting beforehand ran late and I couldn't make it."

I looked squarely at him, realizing my next words could alter my career path for the worse. Despite my fear, I calmly told him I would be happy to offer his apology but I would not be able to offer his explanation. Not only did this exchange offer me a chance to clarify the extent of my integrity, it gave me the chance to test it in the real world. Fortunately I was not fired or disciplined for my action. I want to think my manager respected me more for my action, but since his behavior toward me did not change afterward, it was not possible to know. What was clear was that I maintained my integrity.

Many people espouse a certain value, but they do not necessarily live that value. When we ask them to share a story on that value, it creates an internal conflict that allows them to see the value they are espousing may actually be a desire versus something they live. It allows for awareness and, ultimately, personal growth.

The cool thing about the internal conflict and subsequent growth is that it truly is a choice for you to make. No one can make it for you. I can think of no better way to motivate people to change and grow than for them to resolve to do so themselves. One last in-your-face question on values:

Which of these values would you be willing to lose your job over?

Nothing brings thinking about your values into focus better than loss. You see real values as those you will not budge on; they represent a battle you will fight. In this age of moral relativism, when we often go along to get along, values stand in the face of this sentiment. So what would you risk losing rather than betray?

We have spent time looking at how you view yourself, and now it's time we begin to look outward to grow our self-awareness.

Questions of Perception

This line of questions deals with how aware you are of the way you are perceived by others.

How do you believe others perceive you?

If you don't know the answer, find those you trust to be honest, and ask them about their perception of you. Asking for feedback can be intimidating. Some of us just aren't ready to receive feedback. This is why I recommend asking someone you trust. This person will want to help, not hurt you. I know people who ask for feedback and then, when it is given, are wounded by it and find it difficult to process the information and improve.

Early in my career, I struggled with this same challenge. Over the years, I became more able to receive and appreciate the gift feedback represents. My only advice here is to start small. Get a small amount of feedback from a trusted friend. Consider the feedback; see if there is an opportunity to improve embedded in it.

There are so many examples I can share with you on how this has helped me grow. One important example relates to a time when I was a new manager in a new company. My general manager gave me the feedback that some of my fellow managers didn't trust me. It hurt at first, as I had been trying to build relationships with each of them, and it seemed as if I was dealing with a ghost with this feedback. My manager wouldn't say who he was talking about. Rather than get angry and isolate myself, I made a point of reaching out to develop relationships with each of my peers. Instead of making the trust issue their problem, I took responsibility and reached out. In the end the relationships improved and the trust issue faded away.

Many years later I can look back and see that to be effective, I first had to be vulnerable and trust them. This has become one of the most important leadership lessons I have learned—specifically, leadership is first and foremost a relationship.

Be certain to say thank you when someone has the courage to give you feedback.

What do you make of the difference in perceptions?

After receiving feedback, if you find your perception of yourself does not match the perception others have of you, you have some work to do.

If the relationship is based on a solid trust, the person's feedback will be honest and meant to help, not hurt. It will not be meant to hurt, and because of that, you are forced to deal with the separation that exists between your own perception and an outsider's. Take a step back and see how your personal values relate to that difference in perception.

This is a chance to be honest with yourself and be realistic about the opportunity to grow. Do not be discouraged by the feedback; rather, treat it as a gift, an opportunity to grow and improve.

How would you like to be perceived by others?

This is a question of intent. Who do you want to be and be known as? I believe each of us must have clarity as to who we are and how we behave. When our self-image and behavior are in alignment, our integrity, and hence, our leadership ability, is strengthened.

A small example of this reminds me of when my family immigrated to the United States. As you may know, many Canadians use the phrase "eh" fairly regularly in their everyday language. I recall that when we crossed into Detroit, Michigan, I made a mental promise to not bring "eh" across the border with me. For years now I have not said this giveaway Canadian phrase. Am I ashamed of my Canadian heritage? Absolutely not. I simply realized in that moment in Detroit I did not want to be perceived by others in a limiting way and be reduced to a stereotype. I chose to subtly change my language and hence a perception that others would have of me. In case you are wondering, you can still hear the Canadian in me every time I say "out." Just couldn't change the way I pronounce those vowels!

What steps do you need to narrow the gap between how others perceive you and how you would like to be perceived?

This final question is the real action step of the chapter. Take the time to develop a plan of action regarding how you want and are committed to developing yourself to be true to who you are. Recognize that this is a matter of integrity. When we have clarity about who we are, we can evaluate how we are perceived by others and address any misalignment. We may not see it ourselves without help, but there may be integrity breaches in our behaviors that are holding our leadership abilities back in the eyes of others.

Integrity

One final topic to discuss is protecting your integrity, which is of great importance to work on. You simply cannot be an effective leader if you allow real or perceived gaps to remain in your integrity. Closing a real gap is obvious character work, but what of a perceived gap? Whether you like it or not, others have perceptions of you, and if you are not careful this may include negative perceptions about your integrity.

I recall several years ago an employee telling me I had not kept my word. Alarm bells rang in my head as this was the very sort of message I did not expect to hear. I attentively asked him what he meant. He explained how I had made an announcement to his team that I would accomplish a certain thing. It was fascinating to me because I am very careful with my words. I recalled the exact conversation he was referring to. You see, I make a point of not using words casually, especially when making or not making commitments. Hence, when I did talk to my employees, I would recall promises made.

The conversation he was referring to was a statement of intent given certain conditions (i.e., If X were to happen, then I would do Y). Since the precondition never materialized, I could not complete the intended action. He had chosen only to hear the second part of my statement. I apologized for the misunderstanding and explained why the intended action had not been taken. Several lessons came out of this exchange, which led to this discussion of protecting your integrity.

1. It can be that simple, that people will sometimes hear only what they want to hear. So always say what you mean and mean what you say. Measure your words carefully to minimize chances of misunderstanding.
2. Recognize in leadership roles those who follow you will make "suggestions" that are really action item you have to complete if you accept them.

    Hard lesson here, but do not casually make a commitment and breeze by with a "I'll look into it." You have made a commitment, so keep it. If you struggle with this, recognize the need to learn to say no and mean it. A follower may not like hearing no, but he or she will respect it (and you) more than a yes or maybe with no follow-through.
3. Make minimal promises (which should be made on a level appropriate to your position) and ruthlessly strive to keep them. Who would you rather be known as, the person who lets others down or the person who gets things done?
4. Always tell the truth.

    Truth is the foundation of integrity; we must stay in truth. Yes there are times the truth can hurt. For this reason, always temper it with respect when dealing with others. Remember, our goal in telling the truth is to help, not hurt.
5. Learn to forgive yourself and resolve to improve.

    No one is perfect; our goal should be continual improvement. If you find an integrity breech, take immediate action to correct it and forgive yourself rather than beat yourself up.
6. Staunchly protect others publicly.

    Guilt by association is a hard standard; we must stand up for others publicly. If someone is being criticized and is not present but you are, take action to protect the person. Unfortunately, staying silent in such a situation implies a tacit agreement on your part and hence, guilt by association.

7. Discourage character assassinations and gossip.

   As above, words used to criticize are destructive. Do not be part of them.

8. Own responsibility for all your actions.

   Finally, this piece of advice is consistent with author Steven Covey's first habit of effective people: be proactive. To be proactive means to take responsibility for our actions. Leadership is responsibility, so it is logical that we not look for excuses or escapes. Own your actions and correct your behavior accordingly.

CHAPTER 2
Purpose Mastery

The two most important days in your life are the day you are born and the day you find out why.—Mark Twain

Leadership is about purpose. You see a situation, you see a gap, and you fill it. Steve Farber, author of *Extreme Leadership*, once said, "'I'll wait to have permission to lead' is a self-defeating statement."

You don't need permission to lead, you just lead. See a need, fill a need. This truly is the core of leadership. Our ability to operate effectively in a leadership position is dependent on our ability to observe a need and recognize how to fill it. That done, the step of moving willingly into the gap becomes far easier.

Have you ever been in a situation where there were no clear rules and a large group of people were present? Who steps in to create meaning and purpose in the moment? I had the opportunity to do this at the University of San Diego in January 2009. Attending a weekend leadership course in the Tavistock tradition, for which I had no context, provided me exactly this kind of canvas. Tavistock courses are designed to help participants explore organizational life in an experiential way. Large group—intergroup—processes were structured to create opportunities for participants to study interaction and build awareness. The Tavistock process is a powerful way to build understanding of how people in organizations interact successfully, unsuccessfully, and all the possibilities in between. Coming into such a course without attending the orientation briefing resulted in my attending the course without any frame of reference.

The program started strangely for me, with oblique comments and interjections by the facilitators. I frankly had no idea what was going on or what the conference was about. Moving from large-group to small-group interactions, I found the process uncomfortable and peculiar. In retrospect, researching what the Tavistock process is about put all this into perspective, but at the time it was strange.

Within four hours of starting this course, I identified a group and proceeded to lead them, creating meaning and purpose as we went. Our objective became making sense of the course, and in a way we were fighting against the current of the program to provide meaning when it was being denied by the facilitators. You see, the point of the course was to create meaning individually and corporately. The facilitators were purposely denying structure and meaning, knowing the participants would create their own. Leadership is like that; we see the opportunity and proceed to find purpose and make meaning.

Passion

Bill Hybels, author of *Courageous Leadership*, wrote, "What precedes vision is passion." When you see something so fundamentally wrong, you have to do something to change it. Vision ignites our passion. Our starting point in purpose mastery is to explore areas of passion.

What are you passionate about?
How do you connect to your passions?

Far too often we want to medicate our passions with television, alcohol, drugs, and sex. We were never taught to lean into the emotions that go with the passion. When you're passionate about something, often the emotion that goes with it is not pleasant. I'm talking about passion toward a cause here, passion to right a wrong. Uncomfortable is not "in" in our culture, yet feeling uncomfortable can really connect you to your passions. When we experience a strong emotion, it can be attached to a cause or purpose. It is also possible it is attached to inappropriate things as well, and I am *not* talking about these circumstances.

The question of passion, on a more granular level, becomes: What are the things that make you uncomfortable?

The opportunity to find our passions embedded within them is to lean in, not medicate. If we take the time to actually experience the emotion, explore it, discover what might be behind it, this is what I mean by leaning into it.

What are some of your lost passions?

One of the ways I help people reconnect with lost passions is through entertainment. Many of us are moved emotionally by movies. To discover a lost passion, I often give homework where you must watch your favorite movie.

I have found with many clients that watching a favorite movie will unintentionally ignite an emotion closely related to a passion area. A perfect example relates to the Mel Gibson movie *Braveheart*. His impassioned pleas to the Scottish people to pursue freedom rings loudly in the heart of so many men, including my own heart.

When do you feel strong positive emotions?

Along the same line of watching a movie that evokes strong emotions, our passions can often be revealed through events that bring out strong emotions. Perhaps when you hear a story of perseverance in the face of adversity, it brings joy to your heart. It is crucial we begin to recognize these strong emotions for what gift they are trying to give us. They tell us what connects with us in the deepest places of who we are. Searching for the common theme in our emotions can be a powerful way to discover our passions.

When do you experience powerful negative emotions, related to other people?

Similar to looking at positive emotions, there can be gifts embedded in our painful or negative emotions. It could be that you are suffering from a lack of the positive emotion you identified in the previous section. For instance, you may experience anguish when watching a scene from a movie where people have been oppressed and abused. It is also possible the emotion will be new and unpleasant. Regardless, we need to spend a few moments asking ourselves what the message of this emotion could be.

When are you feeling most alive?
What is going on at the time?

Perhaps you feel most alive when engaged in a sporting activity or debating an important point. When do you feel really dialed into the moment? There have been several times for me. In my current role as a trainer, this happens when I am discussing a crucial point. For instance, when I teach people to listen effectively, I start by first helping them experience the pain of being ignored instead of listened to. After such an exercise I have their complete attention and can speak to the power of what listening deeply to another human being can achieve as a leader.

When have you been taken by surprise by your reaction to an event?

Experiencing sudden emotions is also worth monitoring for the same reasons as above. Whenever we are taken off guard by a strong emotional reaction, we may find an opportunity to uncover a passion. Please recognize that not every emotion will take you to a passion. When someone cuts you off on the freeway, you may think you feel righteous indignation, but it might just be an angry reaction to a common occurrence. Don't lean into this one! It is not my intent to foster unhealthy reactions to common life stressors and events.

The ability to examine emotions from a detached scientific perspective is not always easy in the moment. If you do allow yourself to do so, you will find it is a powerful ability. One powerful tool is the ability to take a deep breath and consider the emotion in a detached way. Breathing helps, really! To examine your emotions from a detached scientific place is not easy. To do so requires us to identify the emotion when it is starting to affect us. Identifying the emotion and recognizing that it is affecting us gives us the ability to remain in a logical, evaluative place rather than dropping into a reactive, purely emotional state.

I had a tragic opportunity to practice this when my mother died from cancer in 2013. In the days following her passing I spent time examining the deep emotional pain I was experiencing. I was aware that I had not experienced this depth of pain before. I was aware of how the emotions of grief were affecting my decision making and interactions with others. In this case I did not and frankly could not stop the emotional reaction, but I was able to examine it and evaluate its effect on me. The ability to do so led to being able to navigate the grief process more effectively and completely.

Talents

What do you see as your talents?
Ask people you trust: "What do you see are my talents?"

Often we can't see our talents because we're so good at something that we don't even pay attention to doing it. When we are effortlessly good at doing something, it is likely a talent. Your talents are an important aspect of your purpose. They are the very things you will be able to offer and do effortlessly to complete your purpose. A purpose disconnected from talents would be a very hard road filled with struggle. I believe our talents are actually critical clues toward the discovery of our purpose.

Sometimes our talents are not obvious, and searching for things ourselves is challenging. Another way to get at this information is to seek feedback from trusted friends and colleagues. Asking the right colleague can reveal talents we may not have been aware of.

Be certain to consider the difference between a talent and a skill. A talent is considered a gift you are born with while a skill something that has been learned and mastered.

There is another term related to talent called "flow," coined by Mihály Csíkszentmihályi, who wrote about this in his book, *Flow*, as related to what he calls "optimal experience."

In which areas of feedback or performance do you consistently receive positive feedback?

There are often times in our professional lives where we are in a flow state or in "the zone," where work comes easily and time seems irrelevant. The work we complete is of high quality and quantity. We are complimented for our efforts. The question is, what are you doing when this happens?

Whether through personal inventory and assessment or the feedback of a colleague, the intent of this activity is the same. Our objective is to collect a picture of our talents. Talents can give us an idea of areas where we may be able to focus and make a difference.

At the end of this section we will come back to our talents and begin to build a picture of our possible purpose.

What are your dreams?
What do you daydream about when you have nothing else to think about?

If we really stopped and thought about it, we may find that our dreams give us clues to our purpose. There isn't a scientific approach to this section, and my recommendation is simple. Keep a journal where you most commonly dream and write your dreams as they come to you. I believe our dreams are often like a trail of breadcrumbs to our purpose.

Connective Tissue

I wish I could tell you connecting passions, talents, and dreams was a straightforward process. It is not. One powerful tool to help connect them is called a mind map. The mind map dates back as far as the third century BC and is thought to have first been used by philosopher Porphyry of Tyros. Mind maps have been used since to create visual representations of ideas. I have found that a visual representation of my thoughts can help me organize them in a way that enables me to find patterns and make sense of them.

A mind map is a relatively simple tool. We start with a central thought and then radiate other thoughts outward that relate to the central theme. Here is an example.

This relates to my recurring dream of being the starting goaltender on the Toronto Maple Leafs hockey team. Until well into my thirties, this dream persisted despite the obvious inconsistency with my lack of skill and talent. In fact, I even acquired goaltending gear and played the position for several years in practices and scrimmages. Unfortunately, I wasn't even good enough to start in a recreation league.

Yet there was a message waiting for me in the details of this dream. The day I mind mapped it, I discovered something priceless. Buried just below the surface was a desire to *support* others in their achievements and share in their success. This was an amazing revelation since I have always acted to help others succeed; this is exactly the type of leader I aspire to become. (Is it any wonder one of my favorite leadership quotes comes from Lao Tzu? "With the best leaders, when the work is done, the task accomplished, the people will say, 'We have done this ourselves.'" For me this resonates with the leader who wants to support the accomplishment of others without the need to be the center of attention, the supportive leader.) The concept of *supporting* the success of other talented people was exactly the core of why the dream stayed alive well beyond what should have been reasonable.

With this mind map identified, the work was not complete. In fact, the "supporting" theme was not yet clear. When I mapped out one of my passions, the elimination of ignorance, the supporting theme became obvious. I took the process a step further in recognizing a talent for communicating and a further talent for learning. It was clear the role of teacher/trainer/coach was an important part of my purpose.

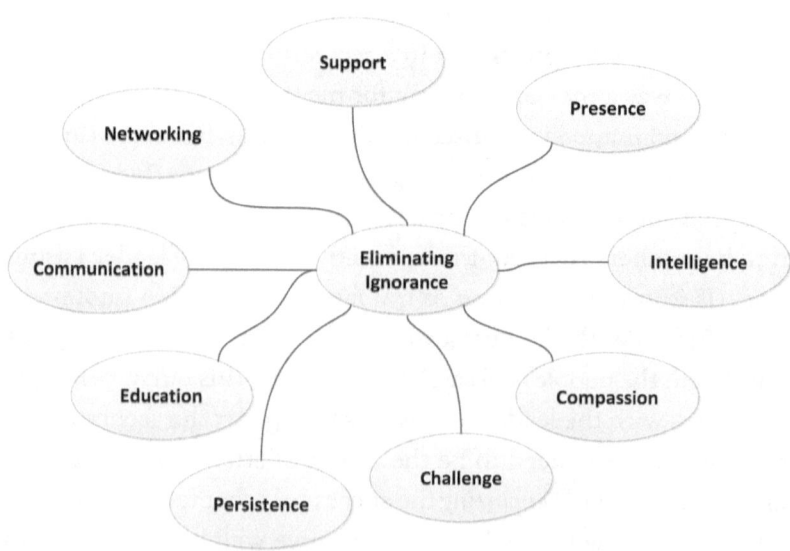

So if you were to mind map your passions, talents, and dreams, what would you discover? To support you in this endeavor you can find a blank mind map template in appendix A at the end of the book.

Recognize that this activity in and of itself may not yet reveal your purpose. To explore further, we take a practical and direct approach.

Purpose

Finding our purpose can be a difficult activity, especially when we are not experienced in doing so. Starting small, seeking out small victories for self and others, is a great suggestion for beginning the discovery process. Actually, finding your purpose would be a worthy goal for an extended leadership-coaching engagement. Our goal in this module is to help you with some of the entry points on this journey of discovery.

This next section starts with the assumption the groundwork from the first section has been completed, specifically that you have identified your passions, dreams, and talents.

What small step could you take today to connect with your purpose?

As the ancient saying goes, a journey of a thousand miles begins with a single step. Often we wait for the right step, the perfect step, when what is really required is a step. The power of the process is found in creating momentum, not perfection. So look for an action that is related to your purpose and take it; do not critique the step, just take it.

Write out a goal related to your purpose, even if it is a goal to discover it. Speak the goal out loud to yourself and any family member who will support you and encourage your development.

With your passion identified, where would you expect to find opportunities to fulfill that passion?

Look in some unexpected places for opportunities. If your passion is something related to your career, seek out ways to give away your time and abilities in a volunteer role. The more we embrace our passions, the more clarity we will gain in how to harness their raw motivational power in our lives.

What steps might you take to identify potential opportunities to use your passion?

Friends and family can be an amazing resource for suggesting ideas and finding opportunities. Asking them for help can be a powerful way to uncover opportunities we never knew existed and gain valuable potential feedback in the process. Many of my clients have used this question to identify new ideas on how to approach acting on their passion. The question is helpful because we can get stuck in our ways of thinking. I say hammer, you say nail. Our thought patterns can become so deeply embedded that we cannot break out of the pattern to see new opportunities. Asking for help allows us to come up with solutions we may not have found on our own.

What is your purpose?

Your ability to lead others is directly dependent on the clarity and confidence to which you can answer this question: How do you expect people will come to follow you?

People choose to follow you in large part due to a transference of hope and value—hope in the future, value in people, which says I can take you there, to our vision of a better future. That place we all dream of going. I can show you the way.

CHAPTER 3
Change Mastery

You can never cross the ocean until you have the courage to lose sight of the shore.—Christopher Columbus

The leader must also master the process of leading through change. Where in "purpose" our focus was in identifying the primary need in the form of a vision, in "change mastery" we transition into how leaders move themselves and their teams through a change process.

Change comes in many forms. Change can happen to us when we are operating at low levels of awareness and leadership responsibility. Alternately, change can be proactively initiated by us when we operate as effective leaders.

Our ability to anticipate the needs of our followers and the stakeholders we serve is critical to our ability to lead change. Leading change is much like walking a tightrope. Go too fast and you lose your balance and fall, but go too slow and external forces push us and we fall. Cater too much to our followers and lose balance and fall. Cater too much to our stakeholders and lose balance and fall. Leaders must learn the process of leading people at just the right speed to maintain a healthy balance and get to the other side.

There is much written about the strategic aspects of change. John Kotter, in his excellent book *Leading Change*, relates an eight-step process in leading through a change (Kotter 2012, 22). His model is strategic in nature and critical to any leader attempting to lead through an organizational change. Each of the eight points are described below.

1. Establish urgency.

   Change requires a reason for people to act. Without a significant motivating force or sense of urgency, no change can occur.

2. Create guiding coalition.

   Creating change individually is unwise. Strength comes from collaborating with a group that can help align the organization toward the change under consideration.

3. Create change vision.

   Clarify what the change represents; where we are trying to get to is critical to success. A clear vision is easily understandable and helps the leader motivate followers to act.

4. Communicate vision.

   The vision must be known and understood by the organization. Frequent clear communication ensures that the vision is not only understood but begins the process of aligning people to move toward it.

5. Empower action.

   Recognize that a leader or leaders cannot lead change on their own. A successful leader leverages empowerment and delegation to create greater buy in to the change process

6. Generate wins.

   Change requires momentum. The ability to demonstrate to skeptical followers that this is not just another fad but rather a sustainable change that the organization needs is critical. The leader who creates momentum helps his or her team begin to believe in the outcome of the change process. In this step we publicize progress, actions completed, goals achieved in support of the change initiative, etc.

7. Stay the course.

   There will be many challenges along the way that will threaten to pull the change process off course. It is critical the leader deals with these swiftly and correctly and thereby maintains change momentum.

8. Embed changes into culture.

   The most difficult and volatile part of a change process is the end stage. We must incorporate the changes implemented into our performance standards, work procedures, and ultimately in the culture of the organization.

Kotter offers wise and practical advice in the eight steps. These are necessary conditions for successful change. The question is, are they sufficient? I would argue no, we need to also incorporate the human condition into the change process. People go through change in ways that must be identified and addressed; they specifically deal with change on an emotional level. Kotter's model is strategic and logical but does not address the emotional aspect of people in a change process. Not only do we need to understand how people experience change, a fundamental understanding of human nature is a great ally. I have found the work of William Bridges and his book *Managing Transitions* to be an indispensable resource in this process.

Bridges relates that as people go through change, they first experience loss, in the sense of something that they value has changed, been taken away, or otherwise destroyed. People react not to the change but to the loss it represents.

When we think about loss as part of change, we naturally have to consider the grief process as identified by Elisabeth Kübler-Ross in her book *On Death and Dying*. This may seem extreme, but the grief process accompanies any loss we encounter. A strange concept at first glance, but change represents loss for all of us. We all fear the loss of something familiar. It may be as simple as the fear of losing our sense of comfort. It could be far deeper and tied to past failed change efforts where people experienced real trauma at the hands of poor leaders. When we bring up change, that dreaded "C-word," some people shrink back in horror or burst out in anger and experience a vast array of other reactions. The successful leader recognizes this is a reaction, and one that, managed properly, is neutral rather than destructive.

The question is, how equipped are we to handle the emotional process? People not capable of dealing with their emotions in a mature manner can struggle to come through a change process in a constructive manner. This is a lifetime endeavor to really master. Let that not dissuade you, since this is the real work of leadership. A leader doesn't randomly change processes and systems. Instead, a leader looks for and implements change where a strategic advantage can be realized. Moving toward what to change requires that we look for the opportunities in our area of responsibility.

What do you see in your area of responsibility that's not working?

A skill of a great leader is the ability to problem solve. Problem solving, however, is a skill very much like leadership itself. It is a discipline, an experiential process, a relational enterprise.

Solving organizational problems is one of three core recommendations I make in all my leadership development programs. (The other two are developing relationships and communicating effectively.)

Our goal of seeing what is not working is more than seeing the symptoms. It is about suspending judgment and diving down to the root cause. Professional problem solvers know that resolving a symptom means the problem will just recur (if actually left in the first place). The challenge of problem solving is, in part, recognizing when you have prematurely limited your thinking.

A few years back I was working with a manufacturing organization to teach them problem solving. Part of the program was to complete a small project related to each participant's work. I asked everyone to write a simple statement about the problem they wished to solve.

One participant wrote, "Our changeovers are too slow and we need a new tool." This became a significant teaching point for the group. I explained that including a preferred solution in the problem statement guaranteed it would be the only way they would look to solve the problem. I asked the participant whether there were other possible solutions. His silence spoke volumes. His approach was to react and fix the immediate symptom as he saw it. His approach closed him off to a number of very effective and minimal cost solutions. In the end he was able to learn a number of approaches to solutions that did not require buying new equipment.

When I teach problem solving, I teach a number of tools designed to help participants reach the root cause rather than stop at symptoms. My favorite to teach is the "5 Whys" technique, developed by Sakichi Toyoda, and was used by the Toyota Motor Corp. during the evolution of its Lean manufacturing methodologies. This technique is elegantly simple and highly effective when used appropriately. We ask "why" to a series of deeper probing questions until we are at the root of the problem. Despite its simplicity I have found many people struggle to use it effectively.

When the tool fails, it is typically because it was used to blame someone for his or her actions. Whenever the 5 Whys technique gets blame, the process fails. For example, if I believe the reason a defect was created is that the employee was lazy, I am done. The next question would be "why was the employee lazy?" This is a stupid question that cannot reasonably be answered.

Rather than assign blame, the 5 Whys technique rightly has a process focus. If we start with a process focus, we will find correctable problems and ultimately the root cause. At times follower behavior is the root of the problem and must be addressed, but this is not the rule but the exception. Most processes make it difficult for the average employee to succeed in the first place, so fix that before blaming anyone.

Let's use an example that brings it to life. Imagine there is an oil spill on the floor of a workplace. We will complete a 5 Whys process to resolve the problem.

First, make sure you have a representation of everyone who might be involved in the room to discuss the problem. Open the meeting by reinforcing the desire to get at root cause and not to blame. Blame focus has the tendency to attract defensive, uncooperative behavior and stall the process. Using a white board or easel pad, state the problem in a way all can read. Be sure to write in any actions needed to correct the immediate problem. Note that if we stop here there is a very high likelihood there will be another spill tomorrow! This is symptom thinking and exactly the type of mindset we are hoping to eliminate.

Questions	Answers	Countermeasures
	Oil Spill	Clean it up!

Next we begin the process of drilling into the problem. Be sensitive to any language that has an accusation in it or seeks to blame or worse, punish someone. We ask the group to phrase a why question related to the answer "oil spill" above. Look again for countermeasures to correct the immediate problem. Often my students say "fix the leak," which on the surface seems the logical action. However, we have not identified what forklift leaked or what the actual cause was. Hence, fixing the leak would result in throwing money at a poorly defined problem. No, our action should be to identify the source of the leak through inspection.

Questions	Answers	Countermeasures
	Oil Spill	Clean it up!
Why was there an oil spill?	Forklift leaked hydraulic fluid.	~~Fix it!~~ Inspect lifts for leaks. (#3 has a leak)

The process continues with the next why, in this case why did forklift #3 leak hydraulic fluid? The response could be that it may have had a loose fitting. Our countermeasure would be to tighten and/or replace the fitting. Again, however, we are not done. To stop at this point will lead to future occurrences of leaks since we do not know why the fitting was loose. We must ask the next question.

Questions	Answers	Countermeasures
	Oil Spill	Clean it up!
Why was there an oil spill?	Forklift #3 leaked hydraulic fluid.	Inspect lifts for leaks.
Why did forklift #3 leak fluid?	It had a loose fitting.	Tighten or replace fitting.

At this point the next why question will get us close to the root of the problem, but there is more work to do. More than ever we must guard against blame and its natural consequence, punishment. Do not allow blame to creep into the process but maintain a detached scientific perspective. We are looking for the root cause, not someone to blame. Perhaps someone, upon finding that the mechanic installed the fitting incorrectly, proposes disciplining the mechanic; resist this suggestion.

Likewise if someone were to suggest retraining the mechanic, resist this as well since we do not yet know about the person's training. Instead, focus on the process. If the employee installed the fitting incorrectly, we need to investigate whether the person was trained, understood the training, and whether the training was effective in the first place.

Questions	Answers	Countermeasures
	Oil Spill	Clean it up!
Why was there an oil spill?	Forklift #3 leaked hydraulic fluid.	Inspect lifts for leaks.
Why did forklift #3 leak fluid?	It had a loose fitting.	Tighten or replace fitting.
Why was the fitting loose?	Apprentice mechanic installed fitting incorrectly.	~~Discipline mechanic~~ Review training records.

Our next question is really important as it will most likely get to the root of the problem. Note that the 5 Whys technique is so-named because in most cases the root can be discovered in about five well conceived questions. If we get to the root in two questions we can stop; it is not mandatory to ask five questions but rather a guideline. Likewise there are times where seven whys are necessary to get to the root.

How do we know we are at the root of the problem? This is an important question that has a few answers. First, when you simply cannot ask another why question and you have avoided blame, you are likely at the root. Second, when your intuition says yes, this is the root of the problem, you are likely there. A word of caution about this approach: To successfully use an intuitive approach requires significant experience in problem solving. Otherwise we run the risk of jumping to simplistic solutions that are merely symptoms that look like root causes. Your best bet is to seek out a problem-solving expert and learn how to drive to root cause.

Questions	Answers	Countermeasures
	Oil Spill	Clean it up!

Questions	Answers	Countermeasures
Why was there an oil spill?	Forklift #3 leaked hydraulic fluid	Inspect lifts for leaks.
Why did forklift #3 leak fluid?	It had a loose fitting.	Tighten or replace fitting.
Why was the fitting loose?	Apprentice mechanic installed fitting incorrectly.	Review training records.
Why installed incorrectly?	Training based on old equipment; mechanic used new equipment during installation.	Update training materials to new standard. Retrain all mechanics to standard.

The 5 Whys process has the advantage of finding root causes in an unbiased way. It requires discipline to help others maintain the same perspective. In the case above, it would be easy to assign blame to the mechanic even at the end of the process. For instance, someone may say, "He should have known the equipment was different and taken steps to make sure he knew what he is doing." Hard to argue the logic of this statement, but I prefer to look at the situation differently. The employee knows the standard now and will make efforts to conform to it. The employee knows he will not be punished for making a mistake and is far more likely to bring a question to the attention of his supervisor in the future. In the end, we correct the problem—now and in the future! The core of this technique is the desire to help the person involved to perform, not to punish the person for not doing so.

There are other tools for deriving the root cause of a problem. Mind mapping, discussed in chapter 2, is an excellent tool for beginning the process. The cause-and-effect diagram is a powerful tool in understanding problems with multiple root causes. Visual charting tools are also helpful in seeing problems within processes. These are, however, outside the scope if this book. I would encourage interested readers to read the work of Edwards Deming, including his book *Out of the Crisis*. This provides excellent perspective on the quality movement and how to create a root cause mindset.

Seeing the Need for Change

What do you see that needs changing?

What we are seeking with this question is an objective evaluation of performance problems that can be solved through effective leadership. Establish what the root of the problem is wherever possible.

Sometimes we know things need to change, and it's not about a performance problem that needs to be solved. There is another aspect of leadership: leaders are intuitive. They see a need and fill it. The need often is that the system doesn't work. Something needs to change or be improved.

Intuition is hard to describe exactly. Dictionary.com describes it as "direct perception of truth, fact, etc., independent of any reasoning process." The ability to perceive without reasoning sounds like a creative process. I like to think of intuition as the ability to see what might happen, what could happen. I have heard it described as the ability to see around corners. I strongly believe the concept of leadership vision is related to intuition.

It can be argued that intuition is a talent and hence not easily developed. More likely, intuition is a blend of genetics, mental perspective, and experience. Certainly some people are born more intuitive than others. However, the other two factors, mental perspective and experience, are also important. I believe that when nurtured, intuition can be enhanced.

Our mental perspective is arguably the most important roadblock to intuition. We need to understand the concept of "double-loop learning" to explain this statement. Double loop learning (developed by American business theorist and professor emeritus at Harvard Business School Chris Argyris [1923–2013]) is the ability to not simply react to the variables and conditions around us but to challenge the validity of the conditions themselves. In doing so the double-loop learner can proactively work to the root cause of problems and apply sound principles in their resolution.

Some people see a situation and experience some outcome as a result.

Consider for instance Bill Murray's character in the movie *Groundhog Day* when he steps into an icy pothole. The single-loop learner builds a reactive coping mechanism that says, when facing the same situation in the future, "There is that pothole again. I'd better step to the right and avoid the icy soaker." So yes, the person has coped with the problem and found a relatively successful solution.

There is more to this example though, since a leader recognizes that others could face the same situation. He could decide to post a sign saying "pothole, veer right," which again addresses the immediate problem. In this case the leader demonstrates a single-loop perspective as well. Ask yourself, as a leader, are you going to be there for every circumstance to post the sign? Unlikely!

The alternative to this mindset is to seek the root cause and correct it so that a coping strategy need not be our reactive response. If we completed a 5 Whys analysis, we would find the root cause of the pothole is frost and winter conditions heaving the asphalt. What then would an appropriate response be? We certainly cannot change the weather conditions, but what of the role of the building materials in this case, or the salt used to melt the ice and snow? Perhaps the town could use sand and not salt to create traction in winter rather than melt the ice. If there was no icy slush and snow, then no icy pothole! Perhaps there is a solution in the road-building materials that would eliminate potholes. Perhaps there could be crosswalks of a different material less prone to destruction in winter conditions.

Solve the problem; don't worry about reactive coping mechanisms. Simply put, to come up with a recipe for every life experience is a fool's errand. Creating a mental model for every situation to make the world predictable is silly to a point of insanity. Understand the principles rather than the recipes.

In my career. I have met many people who have attempted to characterize situations and people such that they could react positively to different situations. I find this to be an impossible task to accomplish. The challenge is, there are often more factors involved than we can see. Hence when a solution works in one circumstance it falsely looks like it should works in many. Unfortunately, the hidden variables often mean the simplistic solution will not work all the time, leading to confusion and wasted effort. It is for this very reason I am a large proponent of leaders becoming excellent problem solvers. The ability to challenge conditions, to ask questions most people cannot see is critical to overcoming the mental roadblocks we encounter.

Our mental perspective should incorporate a clear discipline to solve problems and not allow our perception to be clouded by incorrect mental models or simplistic assumptions.

The second factor is related to the first. To gain perspective and intuition we need to be able to draw upon a deep pool of experience. How do we do this? Live life, be curious, ask questions, and explore the terrain of leadership and life.

What qualifies you to lead the change?

This is something every leader needs to be able to answer. Your ability to facilitate that change will be challenged by those who do not think you're qualified. The question is one of credibility. My best advice to you is, again, experience. The most qualifying factor to draw upon in change is a wisdom that comes from having led successful change processes.

Do you have the intestinal fortitude to see it through?

This is a tough question to answer honestly. Leaders tend to be idealistic and hence are willing to take on challenges that are too big, too complex, and ultimately unwinnable. I think experience is the best teacher here. A leader who has faced the frustration and heartbreak of failing to change a process that desperately needed it knows this is a question we all must wrestle with. To answer the question, honestly consider these thoughts as part of your process. If you fail in your efforts, are you okay with being fired, let go, and/or marginalized? Are you okay with the harm that may come to the people affected by your failure?

I faced a situation just like this several years ago. I asked to be made an operations manager in a critical manufacturing unit. I knew the people and the problem and knew I could help them turn their performance around. My supervisor made me face reality in a rather blunt way when he said, "If you fail, you will be lucky to keep working here." I gathered my intestinal fortitude, took a deep breath, and put my career on the line and said, "I want this role. I know what's wrong, and I can fix it." Such a statement had a way of clarifying purpose and commitment in a heartbeat! The clarity and purpose I took into the role allowed my team to not only correct their performance failures within ninety days, but in the years to come they become a relied upon, respected, and professional operations team.

If the answer is no, you don't believe you have the intestinal fortitude, move on find something smaller to start with. You simply may not be ready to lead at the level you have romanticized. Change is often sacrificial in nature; a leader must count the cost before entering the process. The leaders place themselves on the line, and the followers often must come to terms with the loss of something valued.

Is it worth fixing? If so, explain ...

Some processes are broken for reasons beyond what is wise to address. Sometimes failure can be a harsh but necessary teacher. Some problems have much risk and pain associated with the changes necessary and not enough benefit to make the effort worthwhile.

I think a pragmatic approach is wise when considering change. Ask yourself these questions.

- What is the potential benefit of the change process?
- How much effort (time/cost) will it take to succeed?
- How likely is it people will follow me in the change?

If you find that the energy and cost expended is likely to exceed the benefit of the change and that people will fight you the whole way, the change may not be the best to start with. Start with a smaller change process and gain the experience necessary to take people with you.

Implementing Change

Who are the stakeholders, and what are their needs?

Knowing who the stakeholders are is a crucial first step in formulating how to lead through the process. Dealing with nervous, fearful people, you will take on the role of calming them and conveying care in a patient, deliberate manner. Dealing with insensitive types, you will find yourself taking a goal-oriented approach and looking for openings to get them to reflect on the process. Dealing with deliberate and resistant people, you will find yourself building relational bridges and looking to understand diverse perspectives.

Who is affected by the change?

What do you know of their reactions to change processes?

There is no shortcut here, so the better you know the people affected by the change the better chance you will have to lead them through a change process. Develop professional trust-based relationships *before* you need the relationship to guide them through change.

I strongly recommend that every leader learn about the needs and impact of change processes. An intensive program can help you develop the ability to become sensitive to the needs of those impacted by change and develop healthy constructive strategies to address them. It is beyond the scope of this work to address these issues in detail. However, it is strongly recommended that you do take proactive steps to learn how to deal with the human aspect of change processes. Failure to do so all but guarantees your change processes fail in the long term.

How effective a communicator are you?

This question is a profound one. Most people reflexively think that communication is about speaking; few consider the full context of communication, which necessarily includes listening and understanding.

Rarely do we have objective evidence of our communication abilities. When asked, many of my leadership development program students will claim to be fairly good communicators. On a scale of one to ten, many claim seven to eight. After an intensive beginner-level course, they become aware of what I am really talking about when I say "communication," and their self-evaluation scores often drop to a four or five. The irony of this decrease in score is that it is accompanied by a dramatic improvement in their communication skill. Essentially they learn what they didn't know about effective communication.

As I consider communication, I am reminded of an important quote by management expert Peter Drucker: "Communication is what the listener does." Effective communication is a two-way process: a message sent, a message understood. However, we must realize that no matter how eloquent we are, it is whether the message is effectively received that matters in communication.

How do you gain knowledge of how good you really are? Seek feedback. Probably the best piece of advice you will get about improving your leadership ability is to seek and act on (as appropriate) feedback. Feedback can take many forms, both passive and active. Passive forms of feedback include assessing the visual and verbal clues for signs of comprehension as well as assessing how well people follow through on your instructions. In the table below I offer some examples of how you can experiment with this. Recognize that these clues can easily be misread and require confirmation through feedback. It is best to be a student of human interaction, constantly learning how others interact with you.

Clue	Possible Cause	Action
Work instructions not followed	Person didn't listen	Ask person to repeat what was heard
	Person didn't understand	Evaluate how well you conveyed instructions
Person looking away from you while you talk	Person distracted	Wait for person's attention
	Person frustrated	Change approach; ask how person is
Person rolls eyes and shrugs	You are being repetitive and irritating	Change approach. Understand person's perspective

Interactive feedback is more along the lines of asking someone if your message is being received. Alternately, you can directly ask for feedback about the effectiveness of your communication style.

The topic of effective communication is a coaching subject all its own and cannot reasonably be expanded in this work. It will be featured in a forthcoming Developing Leaders book on the leader's voice.

How do you cope with change?

What's your impact on others as you lead through change process?

How flexible are you during change?

These questions relate to how you present yourself to your people. There is an old saying: "The speed of the leader determines the rate of the pack" (Ralph Waldo Emerson), which conveys the important message every leader must master. As your behavior and demeanor go, so will your teams. Convey optimism, enthusiasm, and confidence even when you don't feel it.

There's an expression: "Fake it till you make it." I'd like to provide warning against this approach. As a leader, you need to know how to take responsibility for your team's actions, and "faking" this ability will get you nowhere. When you are intimate with a change process, there still may be some doubt and anxiety. It is important that you manage your own demeanor and behavior so as not to unnecessarily convey fear and anxiety. In situations where a change process is quickly heading south, real leaders owns the failure and protects their people as best they can.

What steps can you take to become more effective in leading change?

The goal here is to challenge you to commit to a lifelong process of learning and growth. What will you do to improve in this area? Do you understand your preferred learning style? Is it a visual format, audio, or hands on? Most people prefer one as a primary and find reinforcement in the other areas to be highly effective. Translation: don't settle for a traditional class or reading a book if that isn't how you learn. Engage yourself a coach, find a mentor, partner with another learner, or volunteer for a project. However you best learn, get your hands into the process and learn to lead change. Again recognize that the clinical side of change is fairly easy to master, it is the all-important human side that requires true mastery.

CHAPTER 4
Interpersonal Mastery

*Strive not to be a success, but rather
to be of value.*—Albert Einstein

The goal of interpersonal mastery is to be aware of others and to be able to react to others in a positive, uplifting, and creative way. This requires we first know ourselves and actively manage our interactions with others.

I was in my boss's office one day in 2002, and we were discussing feedback some of my peers had given him regarding me. I felt those peers could have gone directly to me and that going to my boss lacked courage. I looked at my boss and said, "They're cowards. I don't want to hear it from you. If they can muster up enough courage to talk to me directly, I will be happy to listen to them!"

He responded with, "I can see you're getting upset."

And I abruptly retorted, *"I am not!"* As the words came out of my mouth, I realized just how upset I was. It was embarrassing for me— someone who prides himself on self-control; I didn't want to be upset. I was managing it with gritted teeth, and when my boss called me out on it, I lashed out.

It's a struggle when your reaction is not what you want it to be but you don't know how manage it. One of the challenges every leader needs to get over and get through is a healthy display of emotions. Some have a head start here; some are more emotionally intelligent and can control their emotions and find appropriate outlets in times of stress. For the rest, here are questions to help grow our abilities in this area: When you found yourself in a relatively emotional state, how did you express it? What did it look like?

Think of a time when you expressed emotion in an unhealthy way.

This isn't about focusing on the negative reaction, it's about bringing awareness to your pattern of behavior. Once realized, you can accept it or change it.

The Power of Positive Thinking

In fact, it's time we talked about positive versus negative words, thoughts, and comments. There are several references I want to bring to your attention on the power of a positive attitude. The list includes books by Noah St. John: *The Secret Code of Success,* and Jack Canfield: *The Success Principles*. Let me also add a classic to the list: Norman Vincent Peale's *The Power of Positive Thinking*. You should also read Brian Tracy's book *Goals*. Each one, and many others, have convinced me of the power of positive thinking. Ancient wisdom found in the book of Proverbs states what I consider to be a profound truth: "As a man thinks in his heart, so is he" (Proverbs 23:7 New King James Version). So if you speak positively about yourself, so are you, and if you speak negatively, so are you.

I am no "brain expert," but it is my belief that our subconscious mind is an extremely powerful computer. Give it the right task in the form of a positive question and it will not stop until it provides us with resourceful answers. Ask a self-defeating rhetorical question and it will agree with us. For instance, do not ask yourself, "Why am I such a failure?" Rather, ask something like, "What lesson can I learn from this mistake?" When we train our mind to assist us, it becomes a powerful ally, helping us through the most difficult of opportunities.

So what is my point about negative words, thoughts, and comments? Simply put, the discipline of censoring your thoughts will help you grow faster.

Yes, criticism is sometimes necessary. I believe it is well placed with the not-so-self-aware, the selfish, and the oblivious. It is also helpful when we are seriously off base and screwing up. However, reinforcing the right behaviors and abilities through positive reinforcement is much more powerful in helping improve performance. Why? you ask? It relates to a powerful little word we have already discussed: "confidence." Receiving authentic positive feedback reinforces our efforts combining our experience with a positive outcome and building our self-confidence. For this reason, positive feedback is incredibly powerful in growing our abilities.

I want to offer another perspective. I know leadership research classifies confidence as a trait, hence it is genetic. You either have it or you don't. That may very well be true, but I have a perspective that I want you to consider. Perhaps growing up you were subjected to external voices of criticism that suppressed the confidence you have in your abilities. After all, if you have not experienced something, it is hard to know if you are any good at it.

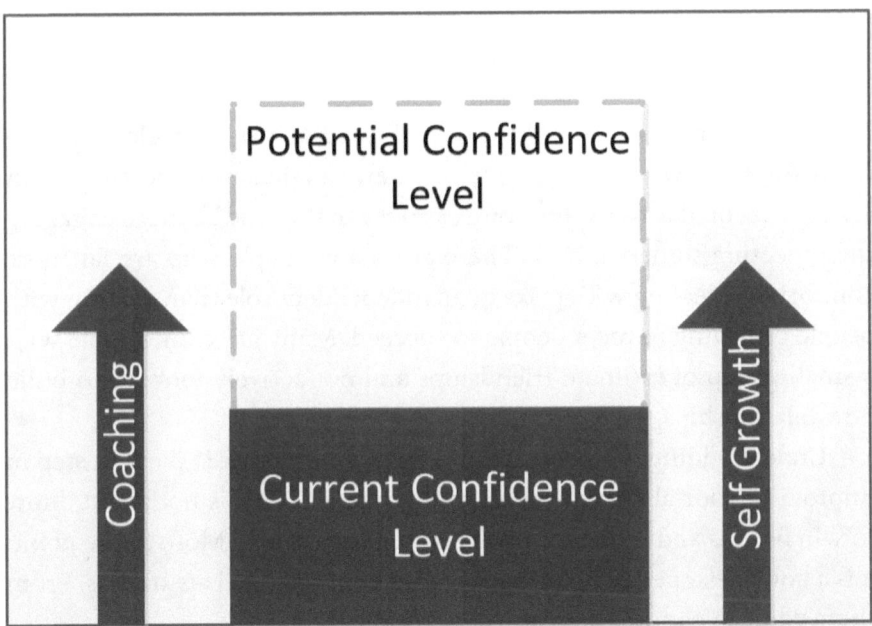

I believe coaching builds confidence. I believe that for many of us, coaching at the very least helps us realize our natural confidence potential. At most, our overall confidence grows. Regardless of the nature-versus-nurture argument, I believe confidence can be increased.

Simply put, positive thoughts, directed at ourselves, have the ability to quickly grow our confidence and leadership capabilities. Throughout this book you will see questions directed at the positive and rarely at the negative. Again, there are times we can learn from a negative emotion or thought, and we need to quickly transform this to the positive to continue our growth.

The Relational Process

How do you engage other people?

How do you go from stranger to friend?

Believe it or not, many of us are awkward at this. Developing new friendships or even meeting someone new in a business meeting is not always a favored activity. For some, a root canal would be more engaging than meeting someone new. There are many people who are far more comfortable dealing with tasks in an independent role than dealing with people or having to meet people to succeed. Many are comfortable with a small group of intimate friendships and not actively looking to build new relationships.

Understanding who you are and how you interact is the first step in improving your ability to successfully interact. This is not about "how to win friends and influence people in ten easy steps." More to the point, it is a book designed to help you increase your personal awareness. From there you can choose to grow.

Do you smile?

I am often amazed at how often I encounter people who don't practice this important skill. In Developing Leaders' program on leadership development, we feature a short module on smiling because it is a crucial relationship-building skill. Master this one, and you will find meeting someone new just a bit easier. Yes, I know many of you do this naturally. If this is you, just skip to the next question.

Developing the awareness of your interactions is important for your continued development as a leader. What can you do if smiling is not a natural reaction when you encounter others? Well, think of something funny and smile anyway. For me this is an image of the minions in the recent hit movie *Despicable Me II*. I went a step further and changed my phone's ring tone and screensavers to minions.

What do you do to engage others?

Funny thing about engaging others—I was reading a great book on communicating called *Conversationally Speaking* by Alan Garner, and he described how many of us wait for others to engage us. We assume that if they want to talk to us they will start the process. There is a fundamental problem with this assumption: chances are, the people we assume will engage us are assuming the same thing! This means the engagement will not happen at all. In Developing Leaders' effective communication program, we have developed a number of practical exercises to address this challenge.

The simplest is to not assume, meaning that rather than making an assumption about some aspect of another person, you ask an appropriate clarifying question and learn firsthand. Simply find something interesting about the other person and ask a question about it. I was at a coffee shop a while back and noticed a man coming in was wearing a hat with a logo I recognized. I complimented the hat and asked about his association with the organization in question.

Find a way to compliment the person in an appropriate way early in the conversation and you will find yourself meeting someone new pretty quickly.

Check out these two scripts and see which version of me you would want to meet:

Attempt Number 1 …

> Me: Hello there! My name is Ron Hurst. Nice day were having, isn't it?
>
> You: Hi … sure? …
>
> Me: Well anyway, I'm looking for a new good friend, and you look like a great candidate. How would you like to go to (lunch, brunch, hockey game, baseball game, etc.) with me?
>
> You: No thank you, I'm busy that (day, week, year) (while thinking *restraining order!*)

Attempt Number 2

> Me: Hello there! I couldn't help but notice the logo on your jacket. Do you work for General Electric?
>
> You: No I don't; my cousin gave me this jacket.
>
> Me: Cool. It's great when you can get quality stuff from great companies, and it really is a great-looking jacket. What do you do for work?
>
> You: I'm a teacher; I work for the local elementary school.
>
> Me: Really? That's excellent. Teaching is such an important role in our society. What do you like best about your job?

And so on.

I am sure you can tell how much better the second script would be in starting a conversation with someone you would like to meet. The last question in that script is one of my absolute favorites that I use almost every day. You would be surprised how easy it is to get to know someone when you express genuine curiosity.

How do you stay in relationship with other people?

In my career, I have found that leaders are often like starting pitchers rather than the closer—that goes for relationships too. We are generally good at starting new relationships and maintaining them over a period of time. Often though when the leader moves on, they cut ties.

No judgment here, just a point of awareness. Be careful that when it is time to move on you're not so quick to end relationships. Keeping in touch can be as simple as maintaining a LinkedIn or Facebook account or sending regular e-mails on major holidays. Reach out from time to time and say hello, how are you? Maintaining a deep and broad network is important. You may never "need" to tap into your network, but the opportunity to help and serve others requires that we maintain relationship with them.

Personal Presence

Do you understand your impact on others?

One of the things I've discovered is that, *generally speaking*, men don't tend to be as relational as women. As a result, they're not as practiced in recognizing visual clues.

Unfortunately, I learned this firsthand. I struggled mightily in developing effective relationships with different groups of people. Part of my journey was to learn from the example of others, both good and bad. When I was twenty-three and early into my career, there was a summer student a couple years younger than me working in my office. We were talking one day, but this guy would not stop talking. I was done, and I thought I knew of a way to shake him. I proceeded to the bathroom, expecting him to take the hint. To my surprise, he followed me in and stood in the next stall and *kept talking!*

To say I was shocked and flustered would be an understatement. Eventually I was able to end the conversation, as I had a meeting to get to and excused myself. It stayed with me though that some of us simply do not know how we are received or the impact we create. This young man and this story became a point of awareness and wisdom for me. Rather than being angry, I sought to help others improve their skills rather than judge their inability.

What is the most common impact you have on others?

There are many possible impacts you could have on others. The ability to assess which one you present is the first step in ensuring the impact is the one you want to have.

Below is a list of possible impacts and the other person's potential point of view in reaction to that impact. Consider which of these you have observed.

Impact	Visual Clues
Indifferent	Lack of eye contact, no expression, looking away
Irritated	Furrowed brow, reddened face, stiff or defensive posture, quickened voice
Angered	As irritated above plus staring, rubbing back of neck, strained voice
Uncomfortable	Backs away, avoids eye contact, looks for exits, faces away from speaker
Comfortable	Faces speaker, relaxed posture, maintains eye contact, natural flow to conversation
Excited	May get closer, elevated and fast voice, smiles, solid eye contact, may touch you
Happy	Smiles, laughter, varying tone, natural eye contact, faces speaker

Understanding another person's body language requires careful study and seeking clarification to be sure you have it right. One of my favorite ways when sensing an unfavorable impact is to simply ask if everything is all right. It is entirely possible the visual clues you are reading have nothing to do with you and may be due to some other event. Asking how the other person is offers a process check that may clarify whether the visual clues relate to you or some other cause.

Our impact on others relates to the state of relationship we have with the other person, our current projected state, and their current state. We discussed the other person's current state above. Our current state is an important one to recognize. By maintaining a positive, friendly, can-do attitude, we maximize the chance the other person will engage with us in a constructive manner.

The state of relationships is also important to consider. If you are interacting with a stranger, there is no relationship to consider, but when interacting with friends, associates, and acquaintances, there is a relationship to differing levels to consider. If the relationship is positive, creating a positive impact is easier to achieve. If the relationship is strained, no matter how hard we try, creating a positive impact will be more challenging. In this case the best advice is, if the relationship is important, work to repair it.

Do you see any trends? What are they?

The first step is always awareness. Once aware of our impact, we have the choice to change our behavior and hence our ability to connect. This is not chasing our tail, though. I recommend you pay attention to your behavior and interactions in a number of situations. Once recognized, what will you do to adapt?

In my new role as an entrepreneur, I regularly take on the role of salesman. I recall one morning going into a coffee shop. At the time I wanted a cup of coffee and was thinking about a marketing promotion, so I wanted to talk to the manager. I was aware of the manager and her positive, upbeat attitude from previous visits.

When I arrived, instead of using my serious goal-oriented approach, which is my base style, I decided to create a different impact. When I arrived, I smiled, greeted the staff, engaged them, and had fun with the conversation as I ordered my coffee. I asked the manager about the marketing promotion several minutes into our conversation, which to that point had been focused on her store, her staff, etc. We were able to connect so effectively that before I left, I was surprised to hear that she wanted me to train her staff. She and her team continue to be my client. What an unexpected surprise to consciously creating a positive impact.

How do you give feedback?

This is the real leadership work of interpersonal leaderships! The ability to give feedback is certainly in the master class of leadership abilities, as measured from the leader's emotional intelligence. Knowing how to give feedback without damaging the relationship between leader and follower is crucial to maintaining motivation and long-term performance.

As an operations manager in a union shop, I regularly had to provide discipline. The curious thing was, I would call the employee into a conference room, provide the person with a written letter of discipline, discuss it briefly, smile, shake the person's hand, and walk out. The union steward would ask the employee if he or she wanted to grieve the discipline. In almost every case the employee looked at the steward and said, "No, I deserved it."

On several occasions, the steward came to me afterward and asked how I did it. None of my employees ever seemed to want to grieve my discipline.

What he didn't realize was the meeting was a mere formality of a feedback conversation that had begun well before. The depth of relationship I maintained with my employees allowed me to have candid conversations with them whenever needed. They knew I cared about them and knew what was important to me in terms of performance. They knew where the lines were and knew I would address them directly, fairly, and respectfully when they crossed them. What was to grieve?

It was about feedback! Feedback is best provided within the context of relationship. Sure you can give feedback to a stranger—you can get punched in the face too—both seem about as smart to me.

Feedback starts in relationships. When your followers know you care about them as people *and* as performers, they will become more receptive to your guidance on their performance.

If you are going to give feedback, there are a few keys that will help you improve performance and keep the other person engaged. First, ask permission to give feedback. Asking the question will help them stay engaged and deflect, at least temporarily, the defensive reaction that almost always accompanies an announcement of feedback. Let's face it. Most people have received feedback, and it tends to be negative and poorly delivered. Hence, people's first reaction is to self-protect.

Second, be certain to give feedback on behavior, not on judgments or assumptions. Remember, people cannot change your judgment of them, but they can change the behavior that led to your judgment.

What is a behavior? If you can see it (body language) or hear it (words chosen and tone used), it is behavior. I also believe measurable performance is a behavior and deserves feedback. For example, if a person completes a project by the deadline, that is a (positive) behavior, and if a person misses a production quota that is a (negative) behavior.

One of the aspects I love about leadership is the more you get to see where others are coming from, their level of development, when you can truly understand where they are and know that their response comes from where they are, the more you can love and understand them and not judge them so quickly.

When someone reacts poorly to a decision I've made, my first response is to wonder where the person is coming from, not to attack back.

I recall a time an employee criticized me during a town hall meeting with all our employees and management team present. As a new manager, it would have been easy to get defensive and then after the meeting get vindictive. Instead I chose a different path—to get to know the person. I spent time over the ensuing years developing a relationship with him, trying to understand his perspective. We actually got to a point where we were friends and he came to me for career advice. Several years later he became one of my direct employees and was one of the most loyal followers I had on that team.

The one thing I've learned about giving feedback is it has to be done in the context of a relationship. When it is done outside of one, it can be a train wreck.

How do you react to emotional stimuli?

In his book *Principle-Centered Leadership*, Steven Covey says, "The only thing we control in this lifetime is the gap between stimulus and response." We fool ourselves into thinking we're in control of situations when we truly are not. The reality is, moving around us at all times is this chaotic mess called life. It's like a giant snowball that can go in any direction, and we put our hand on it every now and then to subtly change its direction. I realize this may seem a little fatalistic but it's not. Life like the snowball above is not something we control, but we can change its direction through our actions.

The only thing we can control is how we respond. The longer you can discipline yourself, to create a gap between what happens to you and how you react, the more time you have to choose your response. The mature thing to do is to choose your response. Somebody offends you, you choose to forgive that person, not react and escalate your emotions.

A number of important resources have influenced my thinking on this topic. Peter Senge's book *The Fifth Discipline: The Art and Practice of the Learning Organization* taught me many concepts about maintaining a learning perspective. It doesn't matter whether you are learning technical concepts, process ideas, or about relationships. Maintaining openness to learning is crucial for personal and corporate success.

Senge introduced me to the concepts of double-loop learning and mental models/roadblocks, discussed earlier in this book. Our current conversation on personal impact is a direct reference to the work of Daniel Goleman and the concept of emotional intelligence. In the book *Primal Leadership*, which Goleman co-authors, I learned of the four primary levels of emotional intelligence: self-awareness, self-regulation, social awareness, and relationship management.

Maturity

This may seem out of place, but it really is crucial to our discussion. Have you ever considered how to help someone to mature?

In my travels I meet so many people who may chronologically be forty but have the emotional maturity of a four-year-old. Again, not my area of expertise, but I have researched this and found that in some cases, people experience trauma early in life that can stunt their emotional growth. They continue to operate from early models of behavior until the wound can be healed and further progress made. Clearly the healing part is more about therapy than leadership, therapy being way beyond the scope of this book.

However, I have found a layman's answer that may be helpful: generate trust. Fear of hurt and loss leads many followers to construct an elaborate defense mechanism. Unfortunately, many poor leaders have helped create this situation through insensitive comments and "well-meaning" criticisms. Perhaps it's a frustrated parent calling out, "You'll never amount to much!," a supervisor yelling, "You are so stupid! Why the hell did you do that?," or a coworker saying, "You're a liar. I can't believe you said that!"

Regardless of the emotional trauma they have experienced, our followers often can't hear us in their defensiveness. It is not until they trust you—seriously trust you—that they can begin to really open up and listen.

You build trust in incremental steps of relational risk. A risk of vulnerability is taken by people ever-so-slightly exposing themselves to others. That vulnerability is held gently and maintained without judgment, and through this act confidence begins to grow, and trust is possible. This process repeated over and over leads to trust beginning in earnest. Over time, you're sharing your life.

How do you deliver a difficult message?

One thing I've seen done exceptionally poorly by many people who claim to be a leader but who really are "managers in leaders' clothing," is to choose an expedient manner when communicating a message: "Oh, let's send an e-mail."

I realize there is much to do and the thought of making face-to-face contact with your followers seems a monumental task. I get it. But we have to recognize that e-mail is primarily a passive form of communication. It is easy and can easily be misinterpreted. Not only that, the e-mail cannot relay how the message should be interpreted. When we depersonalize communication, we abdicate our leadership responsibility. Is this saying there is no place for e-mail? Absolutely not. I am saying leaders must know the role of e-mail in a comprehensive strategy of communication effectiveness.

Below is an example of a potentially volatile e-mail. While not a real example, I have seen the sentiment of this e-mail communicated to employee groups. What is the e-mail actually saying? There are several possible interpretations a reader could make:

- The boss is angry.
- The employees are incompetent.
- The company is in financial trouble (cutting training).
- Layoffs are looming (interview skills prep).
- Employees are being punished.

To: Group All e-mail users
From: boss@company.com

Subject: Employee Capability

All:
Effective immediately, all external training courses are suspended. All employees will be enrolled in a course on interviewing skills to improve their abilities in this area. Recent company postings could not be filled by internal candidates due to a lack of skill by those applying.

Courses start Monday. Check with your supervisor for when your mandatory class is scheduled.

Boss

E-mail is an excellent way to provide written confirmation of a delivered message. It is an excellent way to share data and knowledge. E-mail is an excellent way to confirm agreements and set appointments for future communication. In other words, it is a communication tool, designed to aid you in your effectiveness.

If you have an important message to share, give your followers the chance in a one-on-one or one-on-several format to understand and ask some questions. E-mail closes that door and says, "I don't care about you enough to talk about it directly."

We are talking about interpersonal mastery. We have to be able to communicate in a way that demonstrates, whether good or bad, we are there for our followers. We are emotionally available for them. This speaks to self-awareness, self-management, social awareness, and empathy all at once. Is it any wonder many would-be leaders fall short of correctly communicating difficult messages?

In a situation when you're facing conflict, what behaviors would I observe in you?

The challenge of conflict relates to the ability not to be swept up in the emotion of the moment. We cannot afford to react to a conflict situation when being proactive is called for.

Consider a service business example. Imagine you're a tired traveler arriving at the airport for your return flight, only to find out your flight has been cancelled for some unknown reason. You stand in the mile-long customer service line only to get to a service agent who clearly has had a long and bad day dealing with tired, frustrated, and angry customers.

The clerk looks at you and barks in a computer-like manner, "How can I help you?" No emotion, save for the look of tired irritation from a long day.

You explain your situation, only to receive a "I'm sorry, there's nothing I can do for you" comment. What should you do? You can get angry and yell, thereby ruining any chance you have of getting home. You could cry and plead for mercy, but I don't recommend this approach. The challenge in this approach is it is still centered on you and what you want.

What if, instead of reacting, you consider that they likely are going to be limited in their ability and attitude to help you? What if you start with empathy? "You look like you're having a rough day. It must be challenging dealing with all these cranky customers. How do you do it?"

While such an approach may not get you home any earlier, it dramatically increases your chances. The service agent, when treated with empathy, can relate to you and can move from his or her current emotional state to potentially helpful. For the record, this approach has on more than one occasion not only gotten me home but upgraded!

When I train people on conflict management, I start the discussion by asking how many enjoy conflict. Every now and again a single hand is raised, but for the most part people don't like conflict. In fact, many of us actively avoid it. Our approach may be to immediately compromise to make it go away, to "take it" and allow the other person to step on us, or to simply walk away, avoiding it altogether.

Fascinating, however, is that conflict has the seeds of leadership greatness within it. Think about Abraham Lincoln. It is said his cabinet was made up of the most talented men of his day, regardless of political affiliation. Do you think for a second he didn't set himself up to be challenged and face potential conflict on a daily basis?

Our ability to engage in conflict in healthy ways gives us a crucial skill in leadership effectiveness. Do you really think conflict won't find you as a leader? Really? If so, let me break it to you: you will be a lightning rod attracting conflict. Leaders attract it because in many ways we become the center of responsibility, if not the center of attention. People will inevitably question your decisions and your perspective and will only hear part of what you say and assign a different meaning than you intended.

Here is some advice to keep conflict at the lowest levels, where it is easier to deal with.

Stay open and not defensive. I realize how difficult this one can be, but when we remain open to other people's perspectives, even when they appear critical and possibly hurtful on the surface, we can learn. Further, we can possibly see answers and solutions that would be completely unavailable to us from a defensive, emotional place. The simple fact is that few people are purposely hurtful. It is far more likely they are unaware of the hurtfulness of their words or actions. When we stay engaged and fight off the defensiveness, possibilities open up.

If people are acting in a truly hurtful manner, staying above the attack initially gives us the moral high ground. When it is clear they are acting hurtfully, we can adjust our response. We certainly must stay professional and appropriate, but deliberate attacks can be defended once recognized. I think it important to treat such a scenario as a last resort and expect the best from followers.

Measure your words carefully. As a leader, your words have power—more than your realize. It is crucial you say what you mean and mean what you say. Whenever possible, be certain to leave no room for misinterpretation. You will occasionally be misunderstood anyway. All this advice does is minimizes the number of opportunities. People are funny. We all view the world through our own experiences. If we see someone stuffing a hand in his or her pocket and looking quickly about in a retail store, we think what? It sure isn't that the person just played with the loose change in that pocket, is it? No, we are likely to assume the person stole something.

When followers hear a statement they can relate to, they may stop listening partway through, believing they have heard it before they know what you are going to say. Later they will with all sincerity claim you said something close to what was actually said, but they will likely be dead wrong. Why? They heard part and made up the rest without even realizing they did. The only solution is to carefully measure your words.

Take a deep breath and remain calm. There is something powerfully calming about a deep breath. When we take a deep breath, we practice self-control and the ability to remain in a relatively peaceful state. When dealing with conflict or criticism, the ability to stay calm is powerful.

See the best in others. In the transformational model of leadership, a leader is said to have the ability to see the possibility of the follower rather than his or her current condition. The ability to convey this to the follower is a powerful skill. With an effective relationship in place, the follower will over time seek to live up the potential you see. The same ability is powerful in conflict.

The ability to see the person you are conflicted with in his or her best light will help you maintain a sense of control and peace and will ultimately allow you to stay in a problem-solving, relationship-mending mode. When we drop down and see the darker shadow of a follower, it makes it far more difficult to imagine a positive outcome. In the moment, ask yourself what the other person's positive attributes are. What is the person really good at? When we begin to see the good aspects, we can begin to respect and admire them and see them in their best light.

Offer an understanding response. In keeping with the last strategy, our responses to those we are in conflict with should always attempt to demonstrate understanding. Understanding the other point of view as well as demonstrating empathy enables communication to continue.

As a trainer, I occasionally encounter students who want to disagree with me. They will raise their hand and state, "I disagree with you on this point. I see it this way..." My response is consistent. I listen carefully to their point of view. If they are correct and I have in some way misstated the facts or stated them unclearly, I will thank them, apologize, and clarify. If they have a different point of view but I know my perspective was not flawed or misrepresented, I will find something in their statement that I agree with and respond with, "I agree with you on point x; you are correct. I can see how you would consider my point y to be in error based on your perspective. Thank you for sharing."

An important caution here: the ability to offer an understanding point of view in no way says you have to agree with their assessment. They may be quite wrong in their assessment. Our goal here is to simply help them feel understood as a point in creating constructive dialogue.

This leads us to our last point.

Embrace cognitive dissonance, or conflicting ideas within the mind. When someone disagrees with you and you consider his or her point of view separately from your own, you have two opposing ideas in your mind. The ability to look at both ideas simultaneously is an important leadership skill. Conflicting ideas may connect in important yet unexpected ways, allowing you to find new solutions to old problems.

Most importantly, the ability to hold two opposing ideas in your mind does not require conceding your point of view and accepting theirs. It simply means you consider both on their merits. A mature mind does this with the intent of not missing a learning opportunity if one is wrong in the initial assessment and finding the best solution to a problem. This may mean strongly holding your ground. Doing so after careful consideration of the other point of view gives you an even stronger position since you now know the strengths and flaws of both positions.

CHAPTER 5
Action Mastery

If you don't design your own life plan, chances are you'll fall into someone else's plan. And guess what they have planned for you? Not much.—Jim Rohn, motivational speaker and noted author

In considering this chapter, I was seriously tempted to simply borrow Nike's motto and tell you to "just do it." This certainly would have encapsulated my thoughts on the topic in an elegantly simple three words. Yes I was seriously tempted.

Then I realized there was more to say …

What are the your most important leadership priorities?

What needs to be done?

These two questions begin our exploration of "action mastery." In leadership, we want to be certain we are scanning the horizon and choosing our next priority. These two questions must be asked together so that we maintain perspective on both the present and the future. These questions and many that follow are questions that management scholar Peter Drucker asks in his iconic book *The Effective Executive.*

Dr. Drucker is so highly revered as a management scholar that he is often called the father of modern management. He found that the vast majority of successful executives had several things in common, all of which relate to their effectiveness. One thing I know of Dr. Drucker's writings is that he was one of the clearest of thinkers on what leadership truly is. Not a single training course goes by where I do not quote him. He has been credited by some as saying, "Managers do things right while leaders do the right things." What caught my attention in *The Effective Executive* was Drucker's reference to the fact that successful executives (read: high-level leaders) do the right things, a clear link back to leadership.

So what questions need we consider in action mastery? Glad you asked!

Which of these is the "right" priority?

What is right for the enterprise?

Earlier in chapter 2, I railed against taking the "perfect" next step. I stand by that perspective despite the possible conflict in the question above. Deciding on the "right" priority is an important step in the leadership decision-making process. A leader must be able to establish clear priorities and choose between several seemingly good alternatives, choosing the best for their leadership. Despite this, we work with incomplete and imperfect information. For this reason we need a clear decision-making process that allows us to confidently choose and explain our rationale.

The remaining questions in this chapter were inspired by Peter Drucker although they are paraphrased.

What action must you take in support of the right priority?

What is at stake here is the understanding that it is not what you want to do that matters most but what has to be done. Followers will always look to you for direction, for guidance, for the sense that you know where you are going. Lead down the wrong path by giving in to a desire rather than a responsibility and you will see consequences. We see it all the time: high-profile leaders give in to a desire, perhaps a marital indiscretion, or accepting an inappropriate "gift," using corporate resources incorrectly. If you think about it, the 2002 Sarbanes-Oxley act was a legislative effort to control inappropriate actions by certain organizational leaders.

Other examples are less dramatic in nature: a leader who chooses to skip an important meeting to take care of something less pressing, perhaps a pet project. The leader who chooses some easy task rather than engage in a difficult conversation with a follower to avoid the inevitable conflict is another example of choosing a convenient priority over an important one. The effective leader will always ask: What must I do to move the right priority along?

Recognize that this question and hence argument concede that there will be multiple, often competing priorities. The effective leader is one who constantly scans the horizon for new priorities while ensuring constant scrutiny of existing ones. The lesson here is to constantly be on guard to seek, identify, and act on the right next priority.

There is no magical process for knowing what the next right priority is. How can you develop the skill to find the next priority? My advice here is twofold. First, develop clarity on what your most important priorities are in the first place. This takes us back to the first two questions of the chapter. Clarity on priorities can be built on a solid understanding of the goals and vision of the organization in which you lead and how these intersect your area of responsibility. It is wise to identify what you believe your most important priorities are and then discuss them with your direct leader. Such conversations are powerful in creating clarity of action.

Second, learn from your mistakes. No matter how prepared you are, mistakes in priority will occur. The most important thing to do in the face of a mistake is to ensure you learn from it to minimize the chance of repetition.

A simple and effective model I have followed in my career is to ask three questions without emotion or judgment.

What happened?

Why did it happen?

How can I keep it from happening again?

The first question is the easiest as we already know what happened. The important aspect of this question is to ensure we do not answer in a defensive or self-deflecting manner. If you find yourself saying "so and so screwed up," you are missing the point. A powerful refocusing question is, "What was my role in it?" This question is evasion proof. Ultimately the process requires self-responsibility.

The second question is slightly more complex. It is a straightforward question on the surface but follows the format of a 5 Whys technique. (The 5 Whys technique is the primary tool of quality experts in deriving the root cause of a problem. See chapter 3 for a more detailed explanation.)

The final question—how can I prevent it from happening again?—is easy to answer when we have done a good job with the previous two questions. We identify some particular action that addresses the original fault in thinking or logic.

To bring this process to life, consider the following example. A leader is late on a major project deliverable. This is a fact and can be stated objectively without excuse or blame. Why did it happen? The leader placed more priority on a second project with a later deadline. This answer is not at the root of the problem, however. There was a reason why the leader did so. Was the reason valid? So we ask why again and find that the second project was more complex and required more team member involvement to complete.

Again, this is a valid reason for assigning priority but does not help us. This why focuses us more on what happened than why the leader made the choice. So we need to rephrase the second why question, taking us deeper into personal motives and choices and ultimately to the real reason we missed the deadline. We allowed ourselves to be distracted by an exciting but lower priority project. With this we are at the root of the performance challenge and can address the behavior directly. Note that the solution is not to stop being excited by other priorities but to ensure that the excitement does not lead to overlooking an important but possibly less exciting deadline. Keeping a visual prompt in a conspicuous location would help ensure that important deadlines are always visible.

What Happened?	Late on deliverable of major project
Why late on project?	Focused team effort on second major project.
~~Why focus on second project?~~	~~Second project more complex and required more team resource.~~
Why did I lose sight of first project?	I was distracted by meetings in the days leading up to the deadline.
Why distracted by meetings?	Topic of the meetings was really exciting.
What will I do differently?	Keep a visual performance board on all pending projects and deadlines and update it regularly.

How do you own your decisions and actions?

Leadership is a funny enterprise. We take responsibility for the actions of others to achieve agreed-upon organizational outcomes, often without any sense of whether our followers will do what we need them to. Often there is a temptation to allow them to take the responsibility that is rightly ours when they don't live up to expectations and things go wrong.

When I first took on a role as operations manager several years back, I met with every team leader the first day. I explained that the manufacturing line was theirs to run. I would not interfere but would collaborate with them over the long term to sustain and improve performance. If they made a decision that involved risk or resulted in a downside, I told them my expectation was simple. They must explain the thought process they went through to arrive at the decision. If the process was sound I had their back; if flawed, I would help them correct their logic and I had their back; if reckless, I would still have their back with my manager but they would be held accountable by me. My goal was for them to have the freedom to act … responsibly; there was no free lunch. I was responsible for their decisions and accountable to my manager for the same, and they were responsible for their team's performance and accountable to me. As a result of this approach, my team leaders grew in confidence and in experience. There were times they made a risky decision, but they were able to explain why they had done so. Some decisions worked out, others failed, but we learned from all of them. As a result, that operational unit and those team leads performed at record levels of quality and efficiency.

It is crucial that we take responsibility. At the same time, followers need to know they will be held accountable. This advice is fairly straightforward in the for-profit world as performance management is within the purview of almost all leaders. Unfortunately, many organizations do this poorly if at all and hence tolerate ineffective behavior and performance.

My recommendation? Get really good at performance management, feedback in particular, as this can fundamentally help your performance. Recall that we discussed this in chapter 4. I recommend you spend time reviewing that section and practice giving performance feedback.

The need for feedback is no less important in the not-for-profit world, but our ability to correct in this space requires greater skill, specifically when dealing with volunteers. Because they can, as I like to say, "vote with their feet and leave," we must master the concept of influence to provide corrective feedback in this space.

How do you ensure your communication is effective?

Assessing the effectiveness of your communication is central to your ability to be a leader. What I challenge you to focus on is not your own measurement of communication effectiveness but how other people rate your effectiveness. Here is where it gets really challenging; certainly you can ask others how effective you are, but be careful as it can yield distorted data. People may offer only feedback they think you want to hear. Choosing who you ask this question is important. For instance, ask a peer who respects you. Alternatively, ask a close friend for perspective.

My challenge to you is to learn to read the external framework of how you are being received. Learn to understand the body language clues of communication effectiveness, and the verbal clues as well. For instance, when you are talking, do they give you their full attention or look away from time to time? Do their bodies or feet point toward you or toward the nearest door? These are visual clues that they are not engaged in the conversation with you. Does their tone suggest boredom, contempt, or disengagement? Do their words suggest they are not listening to what you are saying? Are they changing the subject early? Are they eager to end a conversation that has only just begun? There are many visual and verbal clues that can help us better understand how effective our communication is.

I challenge you to begin to build awareness in this critical area firsthand. Get it the old-fashioned way: work for it! Build your level of understanding through an enthusiastic learner's mind.

How do you put your followers in the center rather than yourself?

John F. Kennedy once said, "A rising tide will lift all boats." The work of leadership, as we have discussed, is about sacrifice and responsibility. When it comes to getting credit, my perspective is simple: give it to your followers. Looking for ways to give them the credit, to put them in the center will raise them up and create well-being and a sense of pride in them. After all when your team receives praise for a job well done it directly reflects back on you anyway.

When I was an operations manager, I often had to give tours to important customers or high-level leaders through my area of responsibility. My favorite activity was to randomly introduce the guest to my employees. Praising some specific aspect of how they performed their job, and in doing so satisfied the customer, created two very important outcomes. First, the employee felt valued at a deep and significant level. Second, the guest was given a glimpse into our culture when the employee proudly described his or her duties and how a quality product was produced.

When I was able to make it about the employee, I created a positive atmosphere and a sense of pride in what we did. Knowing I would do this at any time created an effect where the employees tried their best each day, knowing their leader not only noticed but cared enough to share their contribution with others.

How do you look at "problems"?

I mentioned in chapter 3 that problem solving is one of three core areas I recommend every leader master. I have read where some management authors believe problem solving is within the realm of a manager and that a leader should not be problem focused but opportunity focused. Perhaps my perspective is broader than this, or maybe I just see it differently. You see, I believe problems are opportunities in disguise. It is simply a matter of perspective and attitude.

An effective leader must be a master at identifying problems. Those leaders who cannot identify problems are liable to be disabled by those very problems. I look at problems as opportunities to grow and ultimately catapult performance.

As an entrepreneur my early days were challenged, as would be expected. When Developing Leaders Inc. started out, there were only two main customers. It became evident within a few months that one relationship was not working well and the contract with that customer was ended shortly afterward. Complications with this ending led to the loss of my other primary customer as well. Fortunately, a new customer had been added to the mix during this time. For almost a year my company focus was on nurturing a healthy relationship with this new customer. When you only have one customer, you are rather significantly dependent on this business. It is remarkably easy to fall into the trap of focusing all your attention on one customer and not diversifying. Consequently, cash flow tends to be irregular and difficult to manage. With only one customer, banks are not interested in providing lines of credit or other financial solutions.

Fortunately, I had a mentor who had already walked this ground. My mentor was a close friend whose whole career involved starting and growing business ventures. When I began Developing Leaders, I knew he would be a powerful mentor to help me through the tough challenges that were certain to materialize. He helped me reframe the challenge as a potential opportunity. He explained every entrepreneur faces challenges that must be broken through. Doing so typically resulted in a significant breakthrough in performance. This simple explanation and the calm knowing way in which he explained it encouraged me, helping me see the opportunity lying within the challenge. Armed with a more opportunistic and positive outlook, I was able to make it through these early challenges and even begin to look forward for the next one. I took this more positive perspective into every business situation and was able to begin finding opportunities to grow my client base through an intentional value-added approach. New clients led to new sources of cash flow and a gradual smoothing out of the financial portion of my young business.

I won't say I am eager to face serious business challenges, but I am not afraid of them. What I can tell you is that my battle cry has always been and remains: *"Next ____"* (challenge, problem, opportunity, goal, whatever …)!

If you want help learning how to look at problems as opportunities, my recommendation is to develop excellent problem-solving ability where you learn to seriously dig to find the root cause, even when the root cause is your behavior. Such a journey will significantly help you to be a far more effective leader.

CHAPTER 6
Motivation Mastery

*Optimism is the faith that leads to
achievement. Nothing can be done without
hope and confidence.*—Helen Keller

On the Developing Leaders website and throughout our training courses, the second most common question we hear is, "How do I motivate my people?"

I find this question symptomatic of the lack of leadership capacity in many organizations. This is certainly the right question to ask, but because so many organizations rely on the wrong motivational tools, the question remains unanswered.

I conduct a simple influence exercise at the start of every leadership training: people pair up facing one another with an imaginary line separating them. The objective is to convince the other person to come to the other side of the line. What occurs over and over again is that every person will try to incentivize the other person and/or coerce him or her into action (e.g., I'll give you a raise, a bonus, or a day off come up fairly often). They say, "My side is nicer, cleaner, warmer, cooler"—whatever goes in their next attempt. Some try to trick the other person into coming over. All these examples have the same root problem. They look at motivation from the same tired old perspective that in order to get someone to do something, we have to provide some incentive. The concept of incentive as motivation is overused and nowhere near as effective as it could be.

Many a would-be leader surrenders to the context, thinking, *I can't pay them any more, so they are unmotivated and there is nothing I can do about it.* The funny thing about this perspective is how simplistic and wrongheaded it is. Let me ask you this: In the world wars, when soldiers were paid extremely poorly, why did so may volunteer and then serve their countries with extreme bravery? It certainly wasn't about the money. Napoleon once said, "A soldier will fight long and hard for a bit of colored ribbon." Again, not about the money.

As we begin this exploration about motivation, it is critical that you look beyond your old assumptions about money as a primary motivator. I concede only one point on this. It is an option, and yes, a particularly strong one for the person who does not have enough to pay his or her bills. Once a person has enough money to meet basic needs, money as a motivator decreases in overall power.

In my training programs, I often come across people who fundamentally disagree with my position on money as a motivator. A particular example comes to mind. I was working with a group that included a successful sales manager. He was adamant that money was the primary motivator for his actions. The funny thing was that as the course progressed, it was abundantly clear to me and everyone in the room that he was motivated by two primary things. First, he wanted to always be the center of attention, good or bad. Second, he was addicted to winning. It didn't matter if it was an argument, a sport, or a deal, he wanted to win. Money was his scorecard that demonstrated how often he won. Unfortunately, he couldn't see this or accept it when I shared it with him.

There is much to the concept of motivation. Many PhDs earn their rent on the back of their degree. I believe motivation is a relatively straightforward topic that need not be confusing and difficult.

We start by hitting you right between the eyes.

Your Best Self

Why do you come to work?

This is a question I ask every incoming leadership class I teach. I find it amusing that I consistently get the same look as if I am stupid … for the money, they say. Yeah, yeah, but why else? The answer to this question is always insightful and consistent. It gets to relationships, learning, individual growth, and making a difference.

The saddest answer I ever received is one we need to discuss. One young participant said, "Because I have to." I stopped dead in my tracks and challenged this response. He believed that working for a living was a necessary activity for a successful life. In this perspective he was correct. His perspective went further in that he believed this was a mandatory approach, meaning he had to go to work. I explained that I legally earned an income for my family as a business owner, not an employee, to illustrate that there were other choices available.

I challenged his response for what it symbolized. You see, when we concede our ability to choose, it is akin to surrendering our freedom. We become a victim living a life controlled by others. In essence, rather than being the star in our life's autobiography movie, we become an extra. Victim thinking, even in its subtlest form, is a very dangerous choice. Never concede your ability to choose, because when you do you are no longer a leader. Leading others starts with leading ourselves. Leading ourselves means we think and act proactively in everything we do.

Believe it or not, your answer to this simple yet profound question— why do you come to work?—can provide insight into your deepest motivating factors. The answers are what make the difference between hitting the snooze button for the tenth time or dragging your tired, sick butt out of bed and getting to work on time despite the challenges.

What brings a smile to your face?

This is another simple question designed to help you grow your level of awareness of the simple things in life that can provide motivational value. Positive emotions and feelings create an environment where we want to do well; we want to work well with others.

There have been times in my career where I was so goal focused and so repellent to fun that I had to take drastic action. Often I invited my wife to come with me for an evening at a comedy club. I knew that when

I laughed until my face hurt and tears ran down my face I could regain my balance and approach life from a fresh perspective with energy and enthusiasm.

What are you doing when you feel the most motivated?

By now you have no doubt figured out that many of these questions are about building awareness. Knowing what activities are motivating to you is a significant clue. A simple thought is to do more of those things you are motivated to do.

There are a few cautions here. First, I am *not* talking about addictive behaviors; more of those is really not very smart. I am not talking about doing things you want to do at the expense of things you have to do. It is important that we learn to balance the important things in our lives with the things necessary to create success.

Second, recognize there is a significant difference between external and internal motivators. Project deadlines and directives from our boss are external in nature and highly motivating; this is not what I am specifically talking about. It is important to recognize those things that are internally motivating. Internal motivators can be successfully leveraged as needed. For instance, I have a significant internal motivator around learning, which I am certain will allow me to successfully finish a PhD program once I begin.

Third, we need to consider doing things in areas of strength versus weakness. My simplest advice on this point is to never allow your weaknesses to become liabilities while enhancing your strengths. We tend to shy away from activities where our weaknesses are showcased. Don't do that! Get proficient enough in your weaknesses that they do not become liabilities to your growth and success.

When do you find yourself most motivated?

Similar to the last question, we are well served by understanding if there are times during the day when our motivation is highest. Find these and leverage them. We must get to the root of what is causing the peak in motivation. Is it a natural energy cycle, the task we are performing, or something else? Figure out what the stimulating factor is and perhaps it can be recreated in times of lower motivation. Monitor your levels of motivation over the course of several days and begin to see how it ebbs and flows.

When you are aware of a high level of motivation, ask yourself, what is leading me to feel so motivated right now? Over time, trends and patterns will emerge that can be leveraged to motivate you during periods of low motivation.

Who inspires you? Who do you look up to? Why?

While I am not a big believer in the staying power of motivational speeches, I do believe we can be motivated by the inspirational acts of others. As we look across history or possibly just across the street, we can find inspirational stories and perspectives. Such stories can enable us to face situations with newfound optimism and resolve.

A great place to start if you are at a loss here is to read inspirational quotes from historical figures or watch TV shows or read autobiographical stories. One of my favorite historical figures is Abraham Lincoln, the sixteenth president of the United States. I appreciate his persistence in the face of significant adversity and often consider his example when facing difficult circumstance.

This is definitely one of my favorite places to go for hope and inspiration. When I realize others have struggled with similar adversity, it gives me strength. Whatever it is that works for you, get back up and get into the fight. As Winston Churchill once so inspirationally said, "We shall never surrender!"

How do you create motivation momentum?

Sir Isaac Newton was famous for postulating that a body in motion stays in motion unless acted upon by an external and opposing force. He continued by saying a body at rest stays at rest unless acted upon by an external opposing force. Sir Isaac Newton coined this law of physics in 1687. When I first learned it almost three hundred years later, I didn't first recognize how applicable this law was to human behavior.

Okay, a couple of thoughts. We live in the real world, which means this law is operating, and there is always an opposing force—at least two, anyway: gravity and friction. It is impossible for us to escape gravity; the best approach is to accept this natural law.

Friction, though … we really ought to consider this one carefully. There always seems to be friction operating in the life of a leader. This is important to recognize simply because inaction means we will slow to a stop quickly in its presence. It is fun to dream about removing the friction, but this is a significant part of the role of a leader. There is an amazing feeling when we enter a flow-like state where we lead effortlessly. However, that is not the norm, is it?

What is important to consider here is that we must continually inject energy into our leadership efforts to ensure we stay ahead of the frictional forces slowing our efforts. It has been said that when we stop learning and improving we fall behind, and I could not agree more!

The question is, how do you leverage your best, most-motivated self to create even further momentum and become an achievement machine? My advice: start small, get small projects done, and achieve improvement, and you will start the process toward greater accomplishment. Leverage an understanding of what motivates you to push on even in the hard times.

What steps do you take to pull yourself out of an unmotivated place?

How do you manage to achieve your goals in times of lower motivation?

Let's face it. It will happen—days we just aren't feeling it, and our motivation bottoms out. How do you pull out of this state? Having strategies to overcome such days is crucial to the ability to sustain performance.

There is so little positive reinforcement in the world that I believe we would all benefit from a safe, supportive place where what we do well is recognized. My experience has been that people desperately need reinforcement and positive input. The funny thing is that even when many of us get positive and sincere feedback, we push it away or politely reject it. What a tragedy. Compliments and positive feedback are a deeply powerful source of affirming energy that can be drawn upon in times of doubt, uncertainty, and low motivation. The next time someone offers you a compliment, simply say thank you or "Thank you; I will store that for later." Only thing is, *mean it!* Store it for later. Play it back when you need to be encouraged.

How do you deal with fear and anxiety hindering your motivation to perform?

This may be one of the bigger challenges for many of us. Fear, uncertainty, and a lack of confidence can seriously damage our motivation to perform. Understanding your fears is a great step toward mastering them.

There are a few straightforward thoughts I can offer here. First, recognize you are not alone. Many leaders struggle with these thoughts. In fact, they can act as a counterbalance for our integrity, challenging us to be sure of the direction we choose. When allowed to run unrestrained, they can handcuff our motivation to act.

As an example, let's consider the leader who has a significant fear of making a mistake and being called on it publicly. What is this person's likely behavior if this fear is allowed control? It is likely the leader will hesitate in decision making, preferring further data collection and analysis. Perhaps he or she will seek multiple opinions to make sure no one sees him or her as incorrect, all the while not acting decisively. In this example, a leader starts to build a perception that he or she is indecisive or lacks confidence or courage.

In contrast, let's consider leaders who knows this is a fear they have. Rather than being debilitated by the fear, they are able to recognize that has a useful role but can handcuff them. So rather than overreacting and making decisions too quickly, they begin to ask themselves: How much information is enough to support the decision I need to make? They can then use their fear of making mistakes in a constructive way, allowing it to be a check for when they are acting too quickly or too slowly

My advice is simple (definitely not easy, though). Learn deeply about who you are, what you believe, and where your passions lie. It is wise to journal this over time so you can reflect on your growth. Developing deep, clear self-knowledge gives us peace in times of doubt and uncertainty. In my opinion, this is the foundation on which we can begin to build solid self-confidence. We ultimately need to develop strategies that allow us to first recognize the fear and its source. Once recognized, we can then compare the irrationality of the fear against our self-identity and self-knowledge. When looked at from this place, the fear can be recognized for what it is—an irrational thing with little basis in fact not worthy of our attention.

"It's Not about You"—Rick Warren, author and pastor

How have you approached motivating your team?

What strategies have you employed?

Now we move into the meat of the topic. How do you currently motivate your team? Coaching starts with an understanding that you are a capable person. We develop together a shared picture of what has been done already, we explore techniques that work and those that do not. With this in hand we can begin to explore the terrain of what is possible beyond the scope of what has already been done. I said earlier there are innumerable theories on motivation and leveraging, and some can lead to positive outcomes. Overreliance on wrong, ineffective theories can lead to underperformance and frustration.

If we were together in a coaching setting, we could easily camp out on this question and subsequent related ones for quite some time. I have found most leaders have a mixed bag of experience in motivating people. Developing an understanding of what worked and why it did can help us streamline future efforts toward achievement.

In my own leadership experience, I have found developing effective trust-based relationships to be the most powerful motivational strategy. When your followers respect and trust you, they are infinitely more likely to do what you ask without hesitation. Why does this work? Imagine asking a friend to do something for you. What will the friend say? More often than not the friend will do what you ask provided you have a sound relationship. The same goes for followers. Whether paid or volunteer, relationships matter.

Another highly effective strategy is to help people understand the reason you need them to do something. The ability to connect their actions to the strategy and vision of the company in a simple yet meaningful way is powerful. People want to know what they are doing is making a difference. Helping people see how they are making a difference is an excellent motivational strategy.

I present the third strategy as an example. As a frontline leader, I made it a regular practice to learn every role I asked my employees to perform. One time I took part in a safety forklift rodeo. I performed poorly; all of my employees outperformed me, but their respect for me increased since they knew I was willing to lead from the front and understand firsthand what they did.

What steps have you taken to learn how to more effectively motivate others?

As stated above, there are a multitude of motivational theories. Despite the number, there are a few practical and effective theories I believe a leader should embrace. First is goal theory, arguably the number-one theory of employee motivation. The concept here is that we set reasonably difficult yet achievable goals for our followers. Goals they perceive as worthwhile and difficult yet achievable tend to be worked toward by average and high-performing people.

Other very relevant and practical theories include Abraham Maslow's *hierarchy of needs*, which suggests that before a person will pursue a higher-level need, their lower-level needs must be met. If you threaten a lower-level need, they will revert back to that level until the need is fulfilled.

In contrast, *arousal theory* suggests people tend to take action to either increase or decrease their level of arousal toward a specific outcome. For instance, if someone senses a conflict between themselves and another person, he or she may take action to resolve the conflict, hence reducing the person's level of arousal.

Incentive theory should also get a reluctant reference as the one most misused and abused. In this case, we consider that if we want to motivate certain behavior, such as higher work performance toward achieving a target, we should provide some incentive (financial or otherwise) to motivate their achievement of the goal.

What is your experience in setting and achieving short-, intermediate-, and long-term goals?

To better understand goal theory, we must wrap our head around a few critical points. The best way to use goal theory is to embrace the acronym SMART.

S: Goals should be *specific*. Do we know when they are achieved?

M: Goals should be *measurable*. Track progress.

A: Goals should be challenging yet *achievable*.

R: Goals should be *realistic*. Gear goals to employee capabilities.

T: Goals should have a *timeline* or deadline. Deadlines drive us toward completion.

Most of these terms are fairly straightforward with a special emphasis on achievable. High performers prefer moderately difficult goals while low performers prefer easy or very difficult goals. Why? High performers want to be challenged and enjoy the success of achieving something worthwhile. Easy goals are not worthwhile, and extremely difficult goals can rob them of the satisfaction of achievement.

In contrast, low performers prefer to either minimize risk (easy goals) or to face impossible goals that all others would agree could not be achieved (escape responsibility). Need another reason to motivate low performers?

Have you encountered a situation where people changed their motivation or performance based on how you treated them?

How a leader interacts with followers is an important discussion and helps us to better understand arousal theory. This theory can be effectively leveraged in the right circumstances. The theory goes that people act in such a way as to reduce or increase the level of arousal they feel. In some cases, they reduce negative arousal associated with conflict and emotional tension. In other cases, they seek to maximize positive forms of arousal, good feelings, and relationships.

At times a leader will withhold positive feedback from a follower when the leader is dissatisfied with performance. It is likely that if the follower values the relationship, the follower will act in such a way as to regain the withheld positive feedback from the leader.

In other situations, a leader may act in such a forcible way as to introduce tension and unpleasant emotions into a group. The natural response to an unwanted, negative arousal is to attempt to reduce the tension. Careful here, as people may unwittingly act in a manner that increases the negative arousal if they do not understand what is specifically expected of good performance.

For example, I am reminded of a story about a general manager in the technical division of a manufacturing company. The GM was heard on more than one occasion to say he believed people worked better under stress. As a result, he would purposefully introduce stress through means such as rejecting adequate work product and demanding higher quality, or by setting tighter deadlines than necessary or subtly creating conflict between departments.

According to arousal theory, people in this division could be expected to work harder to achieve standards and deadlines in the hopes of pleasing the GM. They might seek to work cooperatively with other departments to lower tension and conflict. The reality was different. While many employees sought to achieve the higher standards and tighter deadlines, this approach often clashed with the previously mentioned goal theory, and employees began to see goals as unachievable and became demotivated. Rather than building stronger relationships, the conflict the GM introduced led to walls being formed between departments, and territorial squabbles became more normal than cooperation in the division.

What has been your experience in using consequences, threats, and non-monetary incentives to motivate others?

This question relates to Abraham Maslow and his hierarchy of needs theory. Maslow's theory is easily the most commonly known motivational approach. In the simplest level of interpretation, one cannot move up to higher-level needs until lower-level needs are met.

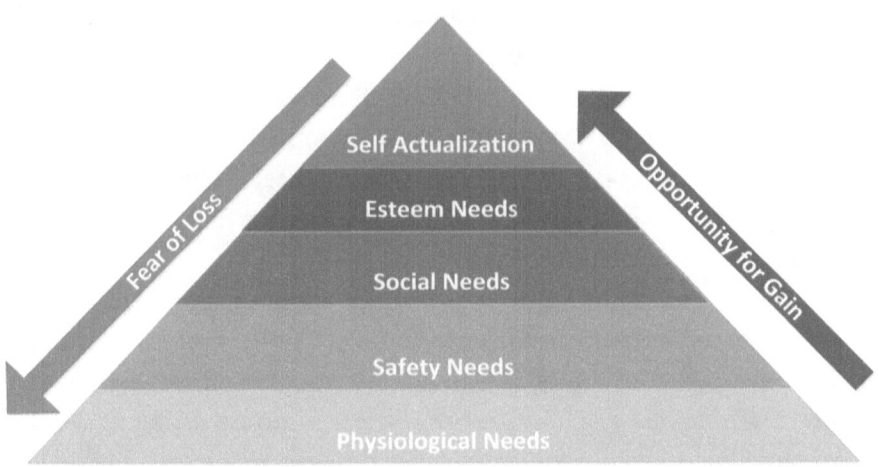

This perspective is generally thought to be too simplistic and that people tend to oscillate between the levels depending on life circumstance. Regardless, the lower-level needs are always given priority. We are strongly motivated to act to satisfy these needs. What happens when a home is broken into? The homeowner, feeling violated (having a sense of safety and security stripped away), takes immediate action. The owner may adopt a guard dog, join or start a neighborhood watch, install a security system, or even chose to move to a safer neighborhood. The bottom line is, there is action.

In 2000 I resigned from one company in Michigan to join another in California. The first several months in the new role were extremely difficult. With no allies or friends, my family and I were forced to adjust and learn everything on our own starting from scratch. On one particular day at work I felt strangely threatened, in the sense that my career was at risk. What if did not succeed in this role? I was actually worried about what would happen should I get fired. Since I had yet to really connect to any of my new peer group, I felt a visceral sensation that my safety and security were under threat. I acted deliberately and consistently over the following days and months to develop the relationships with my peers needed to survive and ultimately thrive in the new position. Looking back, this was a crucial moment in my own development of self-motivation. Realizing I had slid down Maslow's triangle (see illustration above) all the way to "safety" was a true wake-up call for me.

Maslow hierarchy of needs has received much press in leadership theory. I want to make one important addition to this powerful model. It may not be academically correct but it will make sense, common sense. When we as leaders threaten to take away something of value to our employees, such as their job, they experience a threat. The threat is a fear of loss. Quickly the employee can sink to lower more fundamental needs to secure what is of value to them.

Conventional thinking says when we threaten employees, their reaction should be improved performance. While this can certainly be the case, repeated use of threats will desensitize employees to your tactics. Such threats can also initiate a stress response, leading to other potentially harmful consequences. Over time the employee may simply tune you out or worse, call your threat to find out if it is a bluff. Then what? I strongly recommend steering clear of such motivational tactics. They are crude and ultimately ineffective.

Let's consider the other direction: helping employees move up Maslow's triangle. When we do this, we motivate them in a potentially sustainable way, helping them become more secure and complete human beings able and wanting to make a significant contribution. While the fear of loss may be a far more powerful form of motivation, it is destructive, unstable, and unsustainable. The opportunity to gain is exactly the opposite and a powerful way to leverage Maslow's theory for the good of our organizations.

How do you address unmotivated followers?

I am going to offer some clear advice on what has worked for me.

1. Have fun and set a positive example at *all* times.
2. Develop the ability and then treat followers with dignity and respect at all times.
3. Learn to set incredibly clear behavioral and performance expectations.
4. Set excellent motivating goals.
5. Provide regular positive feedback.
6. Learn what motivates each person and find ways to provide what's needed.
7. Explain why their work is important.
8. Find ways to celebrate performance; invent them if you have to.
9. Discipline as a last resort, and be swift, progressive, and final doing so.

What is your perspective on the impact of attitude on motivation?

I have to confess I have a very clear and open bias embedded in this question. I kept it out of the question above, but if you and I were talking openly, I would struggle mightily to keep my opinion out of the conversation. You see, I believe there is a strong correlation between motivation and attitude. I have experienced how a small group with caustically negative attitudes brought the performance of a large group down to embarrassing levels.

I was working with an operations team in a manufacturing company in Southern California several years ago. This team was not performing at the level in which they were capable; they were way below the quality and efficiency goal. I attended one of their team meetings and was surprised by how it went. Early in the meeting an employee, known to be caustically negative, criticized the company, amongst other things. Another employee piled on the criticism, indicating his distaste for how their team was treated. This criticism was followed by the team leader also piling on criticisms. From there the whole team spiraled downward into criticism and negativity and the meeting was a disaster. This team had effectively talked themselves into believing the situation they were in was awful and there was nothing they could do about it other than sit around and complain.

At any point in the process I could have changed the course of the meeting, but I chose not to. Instead, after it was over, I took the team leader aside and conducted an after-action review. What had happened? All the employees were complaining; the meeting was really negative. Why did that happen? He guessed the employees had a lot of frustrations they needed to share.

Knowing this wasn't the case—they had simply gotten into the habit of being negative and complaining, blowing small issues out of proportion—I refocused my question. At what point did it really start to go negative? I could see the recognition in his eyes as he said, "When I complained too." Right.

What could we have done differently to make the meeting more effective? "I can stay out of the negative complaining."

"Excellent!" I exclaimed. "Can I count on you to do so?"

He agreed, and the team started in earnest to move toward performance.

Suffice it to say one of the first orders of business in a new role is to ferret out the negative attitudes and challenge them directly and swiftly to change for the better. The only alternative was the "highway option" (my way or the highway), looking for other employment opportunities.

I have never met any senior managers who would openly call themselves a pessimist. I certainly wouldn't promote people who said they were. The world is full of people who "can't do." I love Gandhi's quote, "I won't let anyone walk through my mind with their dirty feet."

Not interested in being infected by your negativity, pessimism, or any other objectionable behavior.

What we need is people who can do. I often joke in my training classes that I would openly discriminate against pessimists. I have little use for people who prefer to see only problems. The best managers and leaders have a positive, can do, opportunity focus. We see problems as opportunities to improve. We hone our problem-solving skills such that no problem can hold our performance back for long.

CHAPTER 7

Faith Mastery

A leader is a dealer in hope.—
Napoleon Bonaparte

What does hope mean to you?

Author and psychotherapist Dr. Victor Frankl discovered something incredibly powerful during his incarceration in a Nazi death camp, and because of it he became a holocaust survivor. The thing that makes us uniquely human, Dr. Frankl found, is our right to choose—to choose our attitude in the face of the worst adversity one could possibly imagine. This question—what is hope?—is really influenced by Dr. Frankl and his amazing discovery. I think, in the context of faith, a life devoid of hope is meaningless.

I feel this is the most important question in the entire book. What does hope mean to you?

Ultimately, without hope, you have nothing. Hope of a future, health, family, love, or whatever. Where does it come from? What is it all about? It relates back to chapter 2 because what you'll find is that your hope is based on your purpose, and your purpose is based on your passion, and your passion is uniquely tied to your gifts/talents.

When you begin to come to grips with that and know who you truly are, then hope becomes obvious. I would love to see people get to a place where they get why they're here, what they're here to do, and use that vision of a better future as a way to drive them toward the goal, to recognize that adversity and the times we get knocked down are just temporary road blocks to achieving our ultimate purpose.

It's almost like you have to get back to basic principles. In chapter 6 we talked about Abraham Maslow and the physiological needs every human being has. I truly believe the people who are stuck in Maslow's "basement" (what I like to call it) are people who, for whatever reason, have been denied those basic-level needs. Without those needs met, they spiral downward in such a way that they are self-protecting in a place of adversity that most of us couldn't comprehend.

Dave Ramsey, one of my favorite speakers, has a metaphor about why people persist in difficult and painful situations. As a baby with a dirty diaper might say, it may be smelly and uncomfortable, but in the end it's warm and it's mine. We wonder why people stay in pain and difficulty, but the dirty diaper metaphor makes sense. Ramsey believes people stay in pain because ultimately it's what they know. There is something profoundly sad in that statement, but it's absolutely true that we persist in our pain because it's warm and ours, it's what we know. The fear of the unknown is worse than the pain of where we are right now.

As an engineer, I often consider the linkage between the world of physics and the world of human beings. For instance, the idea of persisting in painful situations is similar to how systems in physics change from one state to another. When you think about it, there is a certain amount of energy that's required to pull you out of a bad situation and into a good one. It's just like in physics; there is a certain amount of energy that must be overcome to change matter from one state to another. We must exert energy to change the state of matter, and we must exert energy to overcome a painful situation. Once the energy threshold is met, enough energy has been exerted, and we can achieve a new and better state.

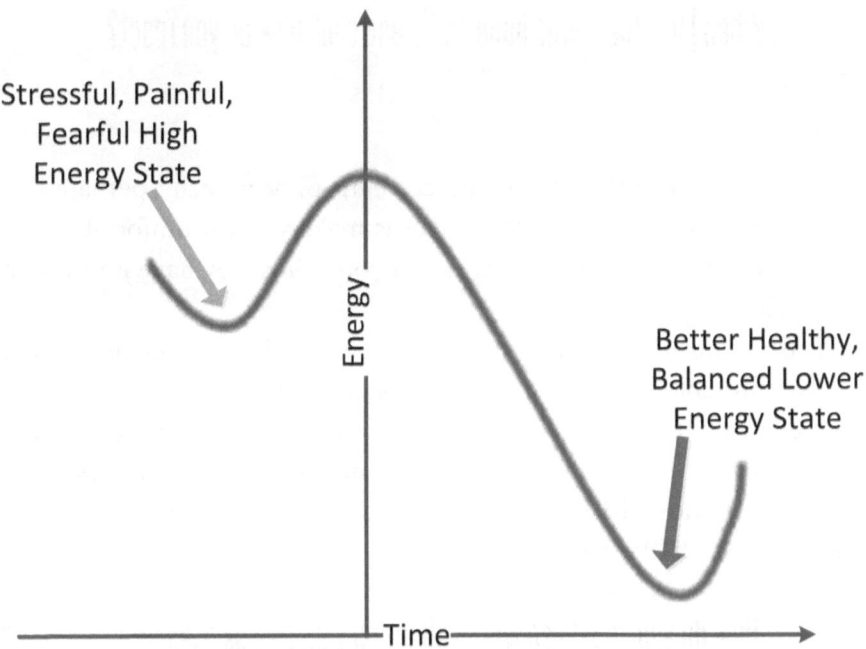

Stressful, Painful, Fearful High Energy State

Better Healthy, Balanced Lower Energy State

Energy

Time

How do you help someone who feels stuck without hope?

An important question, as it links us as leaders to the people we seek to lead. How do you help people who feel there is no hope? Find something that builds a trust bridge and give them something. It starts with trust and finding the one thing that will help take a half-step forward, rather than sitting in desperation. I think they are just stuck, in many cases not knowing there is any alternative. When I was young, my mom used to love to quote a Christian saying: "There but for the grace of God go I." Christian or not, many people believe they are one mistake, one tragedy, one disaster from the exact same place. Hope is a foreign concept to a person scratching out an existence, just trying to make it through the day. As leaders, we represent the hope that followers may not be able to find for themselves.

When I use the words hope, faith, and soul, how do you react?

When I ask you this, do you perceive me to be preachy, perhaps in a "holier than thou" way? Do these words make you uncomfortable? Do they scare you? Do they anger you? Do you think they have nothing to do with leadership?

It is my position that these are the deep work of leadership. These words represent our most important role for our followers, embodying a better way. I believe leaders not only represent and symbolize these words, they act in such a way as to confidently and quietly say, "It's going to be okay. I know the way. It's better there; you can trust me. I can get you there. You'll like it when we arrive."

How do you see these words affecting your role as a leader?

For me, it comes back to Steven Covey, who said, "The only thing we truly control in life is the gap between stimulus and response." We can't control what happens to us, but we can control how we react to it. We can make a choice. In Covey's writing, he said that the longer we can make the space between what happens to us and how we respond to it, the better we have control over what our response is. The longer we have to choose, the more appropriate our response can be.

Our role as leader is to show the way through our words and actions. Our role is to choose our response and to consistently act in such a way as to embody the hope and faith we want others to believe in. As Indian Prime Minister Mahatma Gandhi said, "Be the change you want to see in the world."

What is a follower? What does it mean to be a follower?

The reality of followership is the same as the reality of leadership; we all follow someone or something. The question is, what or who? When we wrap our head around this fact, we realize knowing what it means to be a great follower is an important aspect of leadership. A really important book on this subject, *The Courageous Follower,* was written by Ira Chaleff, who looks at the role of follower from the basics all the way up to a whistleblower. Followership is integral to leadership; in fact, one cannot exist without the other. He explains the crucial aspects of being a courageous follower: to be able to stand with our leaders and at times stand up to them. Developing the wisdom to know when to play each role is the true work of being an effective follower.

I was fascinated by Chaleff's perspective, that being a whistleblower is the highest form of followership. When you realize your leader may not be true to the vision or the hope of a better future you had in mind, staying true to your own integrity and the vision you are trying to achieve can be monumentally difficult. Sometimes it's necessary to take a step in faith and jump into the fire. We must speak out when our leader is headed down a dangerous path.

This has everything to do with hope. Ultimately, everyone is searching for something. Regarding Stephen Covey's book *First Things First: To Live, to Love, to Learn, to Leave a Legacy,* I want to highlight the last part of his subtitle "to Leave a Legacy." Ultimately, on some level all of us want to leave a legacy. What is hope if not a hope of a better future and the concept of knowing you made a difference somewhere? Intricately tied into leadership is the notion everyone has a deep, guttural desire to know they made a difference in this life. Why do people care what their headstone says? Why do they even have one? Who cares? They're dead; they are never going to know. Because it's about saying *I was here; I made a difference. Even if it was a really small difference, I was here; I left a headstone so you will remember me. I named my child after myself—I had a child so you would remember me. My DNA will live on through my son or daughter.* It's so deep within us to want to know we made a difference.

So when we talk about hope, how can we *not* talk about hope? is the better question. It's so fundamental in the human condition. What does it have to do with work? Everything! The question becomes, how do you generate it?

How do you generate hope in your followers?

When I think about this question, I expect some of you will be at a loss for words because it's not a question you are used to answering. It's one thing to talk about vision; everybody talks about vision, since it relates to leadership. Renowned leadership experts Jim Kouzes and Barry Posner, authors of *The Leadership Challenge*, have found that forward looking is one of the four attributes of leadership that never change. The other three attributes are honesty (#1), inspiring (#3), and competence (#4). In their work forward looking, or vision, is consistently the second ranked attribute. So we think about vision, but we don't think about hope. Really, what's the difference between the two? I don't think there is much of one.

Corporate visions don't generally embed hope in them. I think not-for-profits get it right. Their visions create inspiration, as visions are supposed to. Consider St. Jude Children's Hospital: "Finding cures. Saving Children." How about UNICEF: "Building a world where the rights of every child are realized." Finally, Habitat for Humanity seeks "a world where everyone has a decent place to live."

Visions are supposed to generate hope. An excellent vision of an organization should have the outcome of hope. It generates hope by stating and working toward that vision. I get a kick out of people who argue there is nothing inspirational about this company's product, but this other company is really exciting and their vision is inspiring … imagine me with a knowing glance saying "go on" ("you are proving my point"). Visions should inspire us, period. Consider that a company with an uninspiring vision is most likely run by managers, not leaders.

What do you give? Who do you give it to?

What I have observed in my career is that the best leaders are givers first. American self-help author and motivational speaker Zig Ziglar would say, "You can get everything in life you want if you will just help enough other people get what they want." I totally buy into the principle that as a leader, our job should always be to give of ourselves. Leadership is a sacrificial process; we give of ourselves in so many different ways to move our followers toward the vision they have entrusted us to lead them to.

It would be really powerful to take an inventory of where you give and who you give to. In fact, let's take this a step further. An exercise I love to do revolves around people who are struggling to understand what they truly value. The exercise is to pull out your checkbook and see who you are writing checks to. Pull out your wallet and look at your receipts and find out what you are buying because I think you will find that the more you look in those two places, the more you will understand what you are focused on.

Is it about purses? Golf? Food? Concerts? Education? The reality is, what you focus most on tells you a lot about who you are.

Do an inventory and find out who you give your time to. Who do you give your resources to? Who do you give your love to? Where is it going?

A wise scripture says: "When you do a charitable deed, do not let your left hand know what your right hand is doing" (Matthew 6:3 NKJV). Giving should be done in secret and should not be about what you can get but simply what you can give. For me this verse speaks to the sacrificial nature of leadership. We don't give of ourselves for recognition but rather to achieve the vision we have set out realize. So when you do give of yourself don't seek out a pat on the back or some other accolade, do it because it moves you toward the vision.

Take it to a deeper level and ask yourself what the trends or themes are and figure out where you give your time and resources. We all give of ourselves to something. The question is what.

Then there is a deeper question.

Are you happy with the outcome?

I know that is a closed-ended question, and I don't ask many of those, but it is an important one because if the answer comes back no, this leads to an even more powerful question: So what are you going to do about it?

If you were a coaching client sitting with me right now, that's exactly how we would handle the subject. So are you happy with the outcome? One of the most powerful questions I have ever asked wasn't a question at all. It was just, "So?" If you're not happy with it, what are you going to do about it? Giving yourself away to ____ (who or what) would make you happy? What would give you joy?

Let's note the difference between happiness and joy. I really hope I can explain this well because it is a powerful and important concept. Joy transcends emotion. I can be happy or I can be sad, but believe it or not I can be joyful and sad or joyful and happy. I think joy is the deeper sense of being that leaders need to feel when they are totally aligned with their vision and moving in the right direction.

Here's a perfect example. When I think about this business I'm running two years in, and there can be really hard days, on the hardest of days I can drive to a client, teach a class, and talk about leadership. No matter what's going on in the back of my mind, I can compartmentalize it and realize there is a lot of worry, pain, and frustration in this one little aspect, and then I can be completely engrossed in the moment and joyful knowing I am doing what I was called to do.

So I can be joyful and worried, joyful and frustrated, joyful and angry, or joyful and happy (or any combination of joy and any emotion) all at the same time. I think joy is the right state of being. I don't think it's an emotion per se that a leader should strive toward. When you are so completely aligned with who you are and what you're here to do, your vision will be clear and hope will be a natural outcome of vision. Joy becomes a natural outcome from the process.

The deepest questions of a leader are, who are you giving yourself to? What are we talking about right now? If I come back to theory, I'm a big believer in transformational leadership. I mentioned that in an earlier chapter, but in my estimation, when we start talking about faith mastery, there is a deeper version of transformational leadership, and the servant leadership model is the epitome of a transformational leader.

The servant leadership model is well documented throughout human history and is central to the ethic of Jesus Christ, in whom I firmly believe. In Mark 9:35 we read, "Anyone who wants to be first must be the very last, the servant of all" (New International Version). Those who seek to lead others must serve them; it's about giving yourself away. Ultimately, as much as I'm sold on transformational leadership, I'm even more so on servant leadership—and throw "authentic" in there as well because you can't be a servant leader and not be authentic. If you are a servant leader, you will almost certainly be a transformational leader. If you are a servant leader, you will be authentic. The three models are so tied together. Who are you giving yourself to?

Love Casts out Fear

What do you believe about your followers?

Tough question. There are so many ways it can be interpreted.

What I mean by this question is very simple. When you look at your followers, what do you see? Do you see people who are capable and strong? Do you see people who are weak and untrustworthy? What do you see? What do you believe about your followers?

Believe or not, what you believe about them becomes their reality and yours. When we talk about the transformational leadership model—and one of the things I have always loved about the model and something I have tried to live throughout all my leadership roles—is to look at people and see the best.

A guy who used to work for me had been given a derogatory nickname. Everyone in the organization used to call him this name, to the point where he had accepted it as his identity. When I met him, I saw something different in him. I saw wisdom. I saw a caring that transcended the stupidity of that really hurtful name.

I remember one day early on in our time together walking up to talk to him. I said, "Hi, John" (not his actual name), "how are you?"

He said, "John? What are you calling me that for? That's not my name, it's so and so."

I looked at him straight in the eye and said, "That is not who I see when I look at you. I don't see that nickname, which was meant to hurt you. I see somebody who has a lot more potential than that. So I am going to call you by your given name."

Over the next several years we got to know each other pretty well. We became friends. There were times I had to discipline him, and there were times I encouraged him. But in the end I'll never forget that he was a very serious family man. He was a guy who only attended high school. He was a family man who wanted the best for his children. He wanted to give them everything he had not been given. He wanted to give them every opportunity to be successful.

I'll never forget the day he asked me to mentor his son as he entered college because he knew it was beyond his own experience. He trusted me with the most important thing in his life, his son. It touched me in such a deep way that he would trust me so completely. I honored his request and mentored his son. I gave his son advice, met with him, answered some of his questions, and gave him perspective that he wouldn't have been able to achieve otherwise, all the while going back to his dad, talking to him about what I had shared so his father was never out of the loop because it was so important to him.

What John did was so out of character for most men. In fact, what he had to do was to become completely vulnerable to me. In effect he asked me to share a small part of his role as father. Who does that?

It's only possible when a deep trust is present, and he knew I was completely there for him. I cared for him and his family. I wanted him and his son to be successful. He became so vulnerable and opened himself up to allow me that kind of influence. To this day it's hard to comprehend the depths he went to.

When you believe the best about people and operate from the place where they're at their best, you assume they are capable of their best every day and hold them accountable. You love them to the best of their abilities. They will live up to this because they won't want to let you down.

The sad reality of this is that in the lives of most people, no one sees them the way I am describing. They don't even see themselves the way I'm describing and because of that they live by an old saying by Henry David Thoreau: "The mass of men lead lives of quiet desperation." This is such a tragedy. I think the leader's job is to give hope and to see the best in people. What becomes the hope of a better future is knowing I can live up to what this person sees in me.

Now we have to refer back to chapter 6 for a moment and talk about goals. Remember the model I added that said if we see something they think is absolutely impossible it's not motivating? In fact, they think we are a charlatan because they can never get there. So in some ways we have to see their best self—but a sober, realistic best self. If we can get to that place, they will live up to it.

What are you afraid of?

This is a really scary question because no one wants to admit fears. In a leadership context, which of your followers is actually going to come to you and tell you what they're afraid of? I use this line in many of my leadership trainings when I talk about motivating employees, and leading through change in particular. The reality of change and people is this: few people are truly against change. I think most people have an intuitive sense that change is inevitable and they are willing to accept it.

The problem is that change often happens at a faster pace than people can tolerate. They don't have the ability and time to adjust. It's possible they weren't completely comfortable with where things were, so it's difficult for them to move forward. They are very comfortable at the old place, and moving out of the old and into the new gets back to that curve that we talked about earlier in the chapter. It expends energy to get to a point where you can get to a better place.

One other reason people are challenged by change is that they were traumatized by people leading past change events. When people lead through change in an insensitive way, they can end up seriously wounding the people most vulnerable to the change process. The next time change is brought up, that same wounded employee may have an emotional reaction that is almost like lashing out over the way he or she was treated the last time. You see, this employee hadn't been able to successfully move through the last grief cycle. There hasn't been time to grieve the loss of what you now unwittingly asked this person to relive.

It's rare for followers to get to choose the change. Do they have a clear vision of where they are trying to get to? Most people don't. Most people live in a preprogrammed way and do the things they have been conditioned into thinking are the right things to do. And then change happens and they are caught completely off guard. They have been traumatized by change.

I'll never forget the American economy going into a freefall in 2008. One morning I saw a news report about a manufacturing plant in Ohio. A number of employees stood in front of a locked gate, and I could see the fear in their eyes as they looked around and clearly wondered what they were supposed to do now. They had invested their entire lives and careers in one organization. They had been loyal and did what they considered the right thing, only to wind up staring at a locked gate. What hope did they have then?

As one of my favorite motivational speakers, Keith Harrell, says, their attitude went from an all-time high to basement low in a matter of seconds. Tragic because they had no idea what to do; they likely didn't have a plan about how to deal with this.

So when we talk about what are you afraid of, it is important to recognize it is an incredibly difficult question to answer. The reality is people have many fears, and most of these fears are inaccessible by you as a leader unless your people trust you. The only person who is going to share fears with you is someone who trusts you. Why would someone be open and vulnerable with you if he or she didn't know what you were going to do with the information or how you would handle the situation?

I want you to think of people's fears as a delicate and fragile bird. You have to hold the bird very gently. If you jiggle your hands too quickly the bird will fly away, and if you grasp it too tightly you will kill it. It's a really delicate part of the human condition. We have to hold it gently and let them know we can be trusted. If we can't, they aren't going share it with us.

I believe fears are one of the biggest stumbling blocks for people moving into leadership positions, or for people who want to actually follow us and completely buy into following us. What would it mean if your followers bought into a vision of an organization? What could you achieve?

The reality is we hold something back for fear that we are going to get burned or betrayed. I think most people have gone through some level of betrayal. Maybe it was an early relationship where someone cheated on them, or they were let go from an organization they believed in. Maybe someone disappointed them, or someone betrayed a trust. Whatever it was, everybody has felt that deep pain of betrayal.

So what are you afraid of? You, leader—what are you afraid of? Coming to grips with our own fears?

Motivational speaker Keith Harrell once said, "Most of our fears aren't real." They are just made up; they are anxiety based. They are not going to come to pass. If you spend most of your time dwelling on your fears, it will keep you from leading.

One of the things I have learned about fear is that fear has an enemy and the enemy is love. So throughout this book we have talked about relationships and the need of the leader to have good interpersonal relationships with their followers.

There are many forms of love, and the form I'm talking about is brotherly love. The word "brotherly" comes from the Greek word *philios*. Brotherly love is the right standard to have when it comes to your followers. There is another word for love, *agape*. Agape is an unconditional, sacrificial form of love that is also appropriate for leadership. These two forms of love are absolutely appropriate when we talk about how to interact successfully with our followers.

Throughout this book we have talked about making sacrifices and about maintaining good interpersonal relationships with one's followers. If you can master these two forms of love (philios and agape) being sacrificial leaders who give of themselves for the good of the organization, its followers, and its vision, then fear cannot exist.

One of the things as a leader we need to wrap our heads around is that love and fear are opposites. If we embrace fear we will live in a scarcity mentality, and people will ultimately not want to follow us because we will be self-protected. As another great old saying goes, how do you grasp oil in your hand? The more you clench it, the more it slips through your fingers, and that's not the right standard. The right standard is to hold it gently just like the little bird—the fears of your followers. Hold it delicately and teach them you can be trusted—which takes us back to integrity. Keep your word. Ruthlessly keep your word. Love and fear are opposites. Fear is not the right place for a leader. Love is.

How do you exercise power in the context of your leadership role?

It might seem like a strange and obvious question. You might be thinking, *I tell people what to do and they do it*. That is one answer, absolutely.

The reason I ask this question is because I really want to get at the concept of influence and how that relates to power. There is a powerful concept I learned from reading *Real Influence* by Mark Goulston and John Ullmen: "power" is the noun and "influence" is the verb.

I love this idea because power is something you either have or don't have. It's not necessarily how you exercise something; it's just a concept.

Leaders who want to accomplish something use their influence to accomplish the task. They exert influence to achieve their goal.

In a business context, power comes with the title and role. Power cannot be separated from the role you are given. Influence, however, is a skill that must be learned to be effective. Influence is the highest skill of leadership. Earlier in the book I described how relationship building, communication, and problem solving are critical skills to leadership success. If these are the critical foundational skills, note that they all are relevant to becoming an effective influencer.

The opposite of influence is manipulation. How do you exercise power? It's important to recognize that the more we lead people, the more opportunity we will have to provide direction.

What I have discovered is that everyone wants to be led. A great book on leading change is *Leadership without Easy Answers* by Harvard professor Ron Heifetz. He explains the interdependent reality of leaders and followers in change. Followers need leaders to set the vision and move us through the process. However, if the leaders exert too much pressure, the followers may turn on them and remove them from their role. Learning how to maintain an appropriate amount of pressure in the form of influence is critical to leadership success in a change process.

Even I, somebody who espouses and studies leadership, want to be led. I think that's an important perspective because we are always following someone. The reality of most followers is that they will give you a certain amount of autonomy to be an effective leader, but at some point they are going to want to yank back control. If you do something stupid, lack integrity, or make too many mistakes, they are going to want to pull back.

A concept Dr. Heifetz talked about in his book is that as leaders, we are walking on a razor's edge. We need to be very careful to lead well and to provide meaning and hope, like we have been talking about, yet be wise about the way people view us and provide just enough pressure to the system.

Dr. Heifetz used the metaphor of a pressure cooker: you want to put just enough heat into it that people are motivated to change, so you've got to provide just enough pressure and energy into the system to get them to move. If you apply too much pressure, it will explode, and then you as leader will be in the steam. If there is not enough pressure, what happens? Nothing. Literally nothing. If there is no pressure to change the system, people are far more likely to stay in their current energy state and not want to climb that wall of fear to move into a better state.

Leadership is always about the ability to know how much influence to exert in a context, situation, or environment in order to motivate people to move from where they are to the new place, to overcome the fear to move. When we talk about exercising power through the context of influence, it begins to take an important shape and make sense.

To do this well we have to understand how power is exercised and know the difference between manipulation and influence. The tactics of manipulation and influence are not that different, but the results certainly are. Manipulation is often self-centered, while influence is selfless. A key question to ask to appreciate the difference is, who benefits most from this action, the organization or the leader? If the primary benefit goes to the leader, we really have to wonder. Another way to look at the difference is in how people feel when the action is taken. When we manipulate, people feel used and cheapened. When we influence, they feel involved and valued. A good test to determine the difference is transparency. The influencers can effortlessly explain their motives while the manipulators must keep their motives secret to be effective.

It is only when working through influence that visions are achieved in a sustainable, long-term way. Visions aren't achieved overnight, and if they are, they are not worthy visions in the first place. They are just a short-term goal. Vision is something we want to move toward, and we align people to move toward something grand.

Ultimately, this takes us into our next section, leaving a legacy. How do we do that? Through influence. I want to quote Lao Tzu, who said, "When the best leader's work is done, the people say, 'We did it ourselves!'" Influence is about the people doing what needs to be done because they see the importance of doing so. It's not about the leader doing the work alone.

So when it comes to power, we don't need to exercise it. We need to find a way to influence people so they do the work themselves because they want to, and that is what influence really is. Here is the concept. Power is meant to be given away, not hoarded. The more you hoard it the less you have; the more you give it away, the more you will be entrusted with. When we empower people and grow them into a place where they can manage a certain amount of influence on their own, it expands our influence within an organization in moving us toward a vision. So the idea is the more power you want, the more you give it away.

The caveat is you never give it away in a reckless way. You need to learn the concepts of empowerment and delegation. We need to develop the wisdom to recognize maturity within our followers such that we don't give power away to the wrong people. How do you do this? Start by seeking feedback and growing your self-awareness and control.

If you give power to somebody who is immature and power hungry, it will go very poorly and you will end up with a train wreck. Knowing who to give the power to is crucial. Here is a fascinating concept: hire the right people who have the ability to manage the power in the first place and build an organization that is self-sustaining.

I think an organization can become self-sustaining if leaders empower people correctly. When we empower the right people, the empowered follower now adds to the energy input of the organization. No longer must it just be the leader powering the organization to move forward. As a leader replicates this process, we add more and more energy inputs into the organization.

Again, going back to Lao Tzu, as his quote says of the people, "We did it ourselves." The simple fact of the matter is that under the influence of a good leader the people did do it themselves. In the end, the question is about understanding that if we consistently give power to the right people, we can achieve incredibly great visions.

The questions are: What is the vision? What does it mean to the followers? If you can help create meaning and move toward it and help people overcome their fears, you can achieve outstanding, life-changing outcomes.

Legacy—Leave One!

Which takes us to the whole concept of leaving a legacy. The ultimate thing everyone wants to do is make a difference. So very simple question. What difference do your followers want to make? How do we help them achieve this? Rather than starting a grand conversation on the topic, I'm going to end the book with the following question.

What difference will you make?

FREQUENTLY ASKED QUESTIONS
What Is Coaching?

Yes, I know, everyone thinks they know what coaching is and well, yes you do. And yet the model of professional coaching used by trained leadership and executive coaches is different than you might realize. There are too many individuals out there calling themselves coaches who simply tell you what to do based on their experience and model of what they think is right and potentially effective for you. In my travels, I actually call that kind of advice consulting. What makes them think that what worked for them in a narrow range of situations and contexts will necessarily work for you is beyond me!

In the image below we present a model of how coaching differs from consulting. I really want you to focus on the "telling versus asking" row. How do you feel when "experts" tells you what to do? Often they advise you without regard for your individual strengths, challenges, and context. I find that potentially offensive and ineffective. Of course they could be brilliant and have something worthwhile to say, but even that is difficult to accept. The key here is to recognize that when we generate ideas on how to improve with the help of someone (a coach) who is committed to our success, we will flourish.

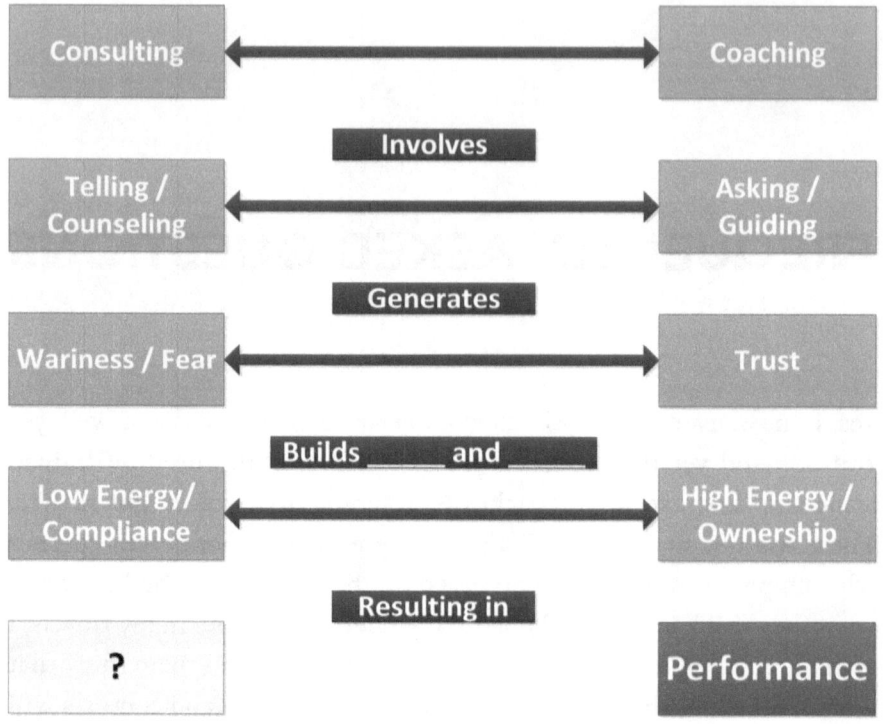

In case you didn't know, you are a unique individual. Your experiences are viewed through your own mind; you make meaning out of your interactions in a completely unique way based on who you are and what you have experienced. No one can tell you how to become a leader; you have to get there yourself. Yes, you can get help, a guide to help you navigate the terrain. No, no one can make you a leader or tell you the exact steps on how to be one. That journey is for you. One of my students said it best: "I will be a leader when I decide to be." I would add to his quote, "and act on the decision."

Coaching in the workplace is not like being an athletic coach. It isn't about training you for a specific role within a team moving toward a predetermined goal where the coach has significant autonomy on your contribution. Coaching is an integrity-based process where the coach's primary goal is your agenda. The goal of helping you achieve your desired outcomes through an interactive yet you-centered approach is critical. Coaching is confidential, trust-based, and client-centered.

Coaching is a process of helping you develop your own sense of awareness and ultimately confidence in your own abilities, all the while gently challenging you to expand your skills to enhance your success. It starts with an effective relationship with trust as a basis and ethics as a compass. Coaching uses deep listening and powerful questions to build awareness. There is a collaborative process that ensues to help you develop an action plan that you want to follow because well … it's yours.

No telling, no expert advice making you feel inadequate. No, it's you amplified—that's coaching!

So now you know.

What Does All This Have to Do with My Being a Better Leader?

Context is important. I don't want you walking away thinking what you are getting is not what you expected. I want you not just satisfied but amplified as a leader.

This book contains questions leaders can ask if they aspire to grow to a greater level of confidence and to be able to be more effective in their leadership capacity.

If you can get better in just *one* of the areas (chapters) addressed here, you will grow. If someone can get better at all seven of these areas, they will grow exponentially.

Why Am I Doing This?

Who teaches people how to be leaders? I suppose you can go to school for it. They teach you what a leader is and perhaps how to be a leader at an intellectual level, but an instructor can't piece it together with substance or something you can wrap your hands around. An instructor can't give you something tangible to exercise leadership. You could also read a book. That is a lot like learning how to ride a bicycle by reading a book. The true learning is in the action, the mistakes, the successes, the execution.

Sometimes larger organizations get it right with their leadership development programs. They blend a healthy dose of theory and context with practical experiences designed to put you in real leadership situations. They work because leading is action oriented. You have to be involved face to face. How many of us get to take part in such development programs? As the old saying goes, "The chances are slim to none and slim just left town."

Do you remember Ms. Frizzle from *The Magic School Bus*? Her deal with the kids was always to go out and experience stuff, get your hands dirty. I love that idea! Leadership is about action and interaction. Without action and interaction, you're not leading, you're just thinking. It's what separates a leader from a philosopher or dreamer.

You Don't Know What You Don't Know!

There is a really simple model that we need to discuss. The model describes how people learn. This is important because once you understand and embrace it, the model provides for a higher level of empowerment to the learner.

All learning starts in a place of ignorance; stated another way, we don't know what we don't know. How can you learn something when you don't know the concept even exists? The movement between not knowing, or unconscious incompetence, to knowing, or conscious incompetence, is the process where awareness occurs. This is represented in the picture below when we move from the bottom right to the upper right box.

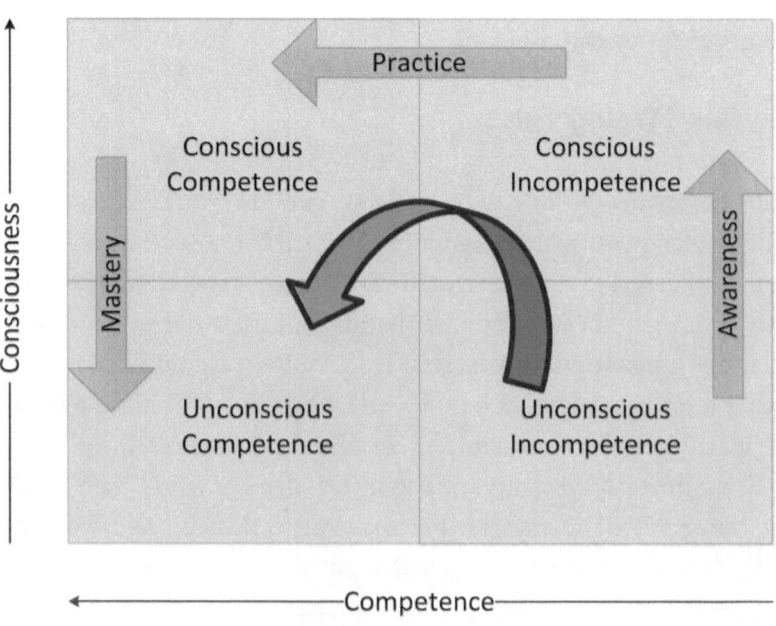

This is the starting point of learning! When we become aware of something we do not know, we have a choice to ignore the opportunity to learn and sink back into ignorance or to embrace the opportunity. When we choose to discover and learn, this is an exciting moment. There is a certain humility required here, a humility that most high-performing leaders I have known embraced.

Recognizing something must be learned often requires an unlearning or letting go of some older perception or knowledge. Letting go is not always an easy process since we often tie our knowledge to our identity. The ability to look at learning opportunities as independent events separate from our identity and a chance to grow is an important decision to make. Those who make this choice can begin to learn.

The process of learning often involves awkwardness, not unlike learning to ride a bicycle. We try new things, make mistakes, and learn from them, and if we are persistent, we gain new abilities. We may not be experts yet, but the process of practicing a new skill is what moves us from consciously incompetent to consciously competent in our learning model.

Continued practice of the new skill or ability eventually leads to a state where we no longer need to expend conscious energy to produce the ability; our subconscious mind does the work. When we arrive here we are in a state of mastery or unconscious competence.

A practical side note and reference to our previous discussion on born leaders relates to this point. In a sense, people born with leadership abilities are the wrong ones to teach you how to become a leader. If people have not gone through the journey of learning, it will be difficult for them to describe how to help you learn. Simply put, they haven't walked the ground, so they cannot describe the terrain.

What you need is someone who has learned the way, from trial and error, scratching and clawing their way toward mastery, that you are about to undertake. Such leaders will not only have the needed wisdom but the empathy to help you along.

What If I Want to Go Further in My Development?

If you want to go further, you will have to reach out and take the risk of hiring a leadership coach. Together you will explore who you are as a leader and co-create a plan for your next steps in leadership development you can walk in.

If you want more information on hiring a leadership coach, contact us at info@developingleaders.co.

APPENDIX A
Mind Map Template

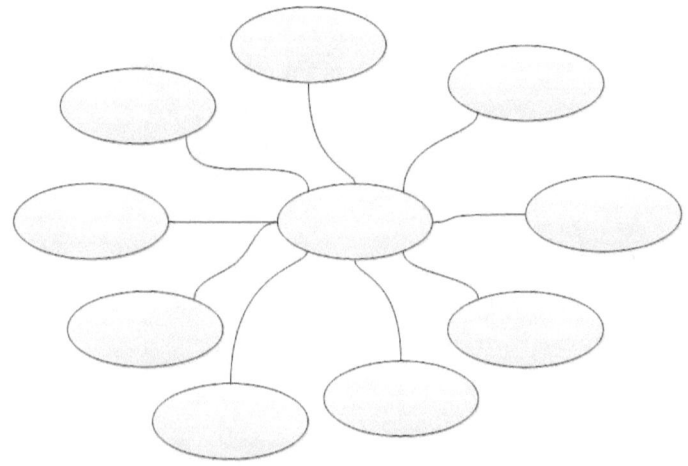

APPENDIX A

Bibliography

Bridges, W. *Managing Transitions: Making the Most of Change*, Philadelphia, PA: Da Capo Lifelong, 2009.

Buckingham, M. and Curt Coffman. *First, Break All the Rules: What the World's Greatest Managers Do Differently*, New York, NY: Simon & Schuster, 1999.

Canfield, J. and Janet Switzer. *The Success Principles: How to Get from Where You Are to Where You Want to Be*, New York: Collins, 2007.

Cashman, K. *Leadership from the inside Out: Becoming a Leader for Life*, San Francisco, CA: Berrett-Koehler, 2008.

Chaleff, I. *The Courageous Follower: Standing up to and for Our Leaders*, San Francisco: Berrett-Koehler, 2009.

Covey, S., Rebecca R. Merrill, and A. Roger Merrill. *First Things First*, New York: Fireside Book, 1994.

Covey, S. *Principle-Centered leadership*, London: Simon & Schuster, 1999.

Csikszentmihalyi, M. *Flow: The Psychology of Optimal Experience*, New York: Harper Perennial, 2008.

Deming, W. E. *Out of the Crisis*, Cambridge, MA: MIT, 2000.

Drucker, P. F. *The Effective Executive: The Definitive Guide to Getting the Right Things Done,* New York: Collins, 2006.

Frankl, V. *Man's Search for Meaning,* Boston, MA: Beacon, 2006.

Garner, A. *Conversationally Speaking: Tested New Ways to Increase Your Personal and Social Effectiveness,* newly rev. 3rd ed. Los Angeles: Lowell House, 1997.

Holy Bible, The. *New International Version,* Grand Rapids, MI: Zondervan, 2005.

Holy Bible, The. *New King James Version,* Nashville, TN: Nelson Bibles, 1982.

Goldsmith, M. and Mark Reiter. *What Got You Here Won't Get You There: How Successful People Become Even More Successful,* New York, NY: Hyperion, 2007.

Goleman, D., Richard E. Boyatzis, and Annie McKee. *Primal Leadership: Learning to Lead with Emotional Intelligence,* Boston, MA: Harvard Business School, 2004.

Goulston, M. and John B. Ullmen. *Real Influence: Persuade without Pushing and Gain without Giving In,* New York: American Management Association, 2012.

Heifetz, R. A. *Leadership without Easy Answers,* Cambridge, MA: Belknap of Harvard UP, 1994.

Hybels, B. *Courageous Leadership,* Grand Rapids: Zondervan, 2012.

Katz, R. L. "Skills of an Effective Administrator," *Harvard Business Review.* Mar 1956.

Kotter, J. P. *Leading Change,* Boston: Harvard Business Review, 2012.

Kouzes, J. M. and Barry Z. Posner. *The Leadership Challenge: How to Make Extraordinary Things Happen in Organizations,* San Francisco, CA: Jossey-Bass, 2012.

Kübler-Ross, E. *On Death and Dying,* New York: Touchstone, 1969.

Peale, N. V. *The Power of Positive Thinking,* New York: Fireside/Simon & Schuster, 2003.

Peter, L. J. and Raymond Hull. *The Peter Principle,* New York: W. Morrow, 1969.

Senge, P. M. *The Fifth Discipline: The Art and Practice of the Learning Organization,* New York: Doubleday/Currency, 2006.

St. John, N. *The Secret Code of Success: 7 Hidden Steps to More Wealth and Happiness,* New York: HarperCollins, 2009.

Tracy, B. *Goals! How to Get Everything You Want, Faster than You Ever Thought Possible,* 2nd ed. San Francisco: Berrett-Koehler Publishers, 2010.

Ziglar, Z. *Secrets of Closing the Sale,* Grand Rapids, MI: Fleming H. Revell Co., 1984.

About the Author

Ron Hurst is an experienced manufacturing manager and president of Developing Leaders Incorporated. He holds master's degrees in leadership and organizational development as well as in business administration and is currently pursuing a PhD in organizational psychology. Ron is certified through the International Coaching Federation. He lives in Fontana, California, with his wife, their children, and their dog.